OSPREY
PUBLISHING

Vietnam ANZ

Australian & New Zealar

in Vietnam 1962–72

Kevin Lyles

First published in Great Britain in 2004 by Osprey Publishing
Elms Court, Chapel Way, Botley, Oxford OX2 9LP, United Kingdom
Email: info@ospreypublishing.com

A CIP catalogue record for this title is available from the British Library.

ISBN 1 84176 702 6

Editor: Martin Windrow
Design: Alan Hamp
Index by Glyn Sutcliffe
Originated by Grasmere Digital Imaging, Leeds, UK
Printed in China through World Print Ltd.

04 05 06 07 08 10 9 8 7 6 5 4 3 2 1

FOR A CATALOGUE OF ALL BOOKS PUBLISHED BY
OSPREY MILITARY AND AVIATION PLEASE CONTACT:

The Marketing Manager, Osprey Direct UK
PO Box 140, Wellingborough, Northants, NN8 2FA, United Kingdom
Email: info@ospreydirect.co.uk

The Marketing Manager, Osprey Direct USA, c/o MBI Publishing
729 Prospect Avenue, Osceola, WI 54020, USA
Email: info@ospreydirectusa.com

www.ospreypublishing.com

Author's Note & Acknowledgements

This modest volume represents the fruits of some ten years of research into the Australian and New Zealand soldier in Vietnam, and was born out of simple frustration. The few published works that mentioned the ANZACs promoted the idea that they were dressed and equipped with a random mix of hand-me-down British and American gear – obviously a simplistic and slightly offensive notion. Hopefully this book will go some way to setting the record straight. Because of the long range nature of the research, even more reliance than usual was placed on the assistance of friends and colleagues in both Australia and New Zealand, and I would like to record my sincere thanks here. This project would have been doomed to failure without the considerable input of the following, whether veterans, museum staff or researchers: Peter Aitken, Greg Amey, Evan Black, Kevin Bovill, Ben Cox, Jim Deadman, Simon Dunstan, Ian Kuring, Rick Landers, Shane Lovell, Noel Luff, Robert Miles, Neville Modystack, Gary Oakley, Colin Smith; and the Director of the Australian War Memorial, Canberra.

Artist's Note

Readers may care to note that the original paintings from which the colour plates in this book were prepared are available for private sale. All reproduction copyright whatsoever is retained by the Publishers. All enquiries should be addressed to:

Kevin Lyles, 10 Cow Roast, Tring, Herts HP23 5RF

The Publishers regret that they can enter into no correspondence upon this matter.

VIETNAM ANZACs 1962–72

INTRODUCTION

'**A**NZAC' IS THE ACRONYM for the Australian and New Zealand Army Corps, originally coined when troops of the two neighbouring nations first fought together in combined formations in 1915. From the title of an official military organization it has become the colloquial collective term for all Australian and New Zealand servicemen – 'Diggers' and 'Kiwis' – when serving side by side. 'Anzac' is used in that sense throughout this text, except where capitalized as the specific title of joint Australian/New Zealand infantry 'ANZAC Battalions'.

* * *

Australia's involvement in the Vietnam War began on 3 August 1962, with the low-key arrival at Saigon-Tan Son Nhut airport of 30 military advisers. This small group represented the vanguard of close to 50,000 Australian servicemen who would serve in Vietnam over the next decade. Set against the huge American troop deployments the Australian contingent was relatively small – a little over 8,000 strong at its peak in 1968. However, the Diggers and later New Zealanders were to establish a reputation for professionalism and effective soldiering unrivalled in Vietnam.

From the outset the US government was keen that its efforts in South Vietnam were seen as part of a multi-national opposition to Communism in the region. To counter claims that American 'imperialism' had merely replaced French colonialism in Indochina, the US wanted the support of other 'Free World' nations. In April 1964 President Lyndon B.Johnson called for 'more flags' to be represented in the growing struggle in South Vietnam. Australia's decision to respond to this request was motivated partly by a desire to come to the aid of an old ally, and partly in pursuit of her current strategy of 'Forward Defence' against the spread of Communism in South-East Asia.

Bien Hoa, May 1965: a sergeant of 1RAR and an American Pfc of 173rd Abn Bde examine the latter's M16 rifle. The slouch hat was such a proud mark of the Australian soldier that it was worn for any event with 'public relations' value, especially in the early days of 1RAR's first tour; the down-turned brim was an active service privilege. Note the Australian Military Forces patch on the left shoulder; white-on-brown rank chevrons on both sleeves; and the Owen gun just visible on the sergeant's lap – soon to be superseded by the M16. (Unless otherwise credited, all photographs are courtesy Australian War Memorial, Canberra)

In the early 1960s the governments of both Australia and New Zealand subscribed to President Eisenhower's 'Domino Theory', in which the dominos symbolized the countries of Asia falling one by one to the forces of Communism. Within this context Australian and New Zealand forces had fought continuously for 17 years against Communist-backed aggression in the region. During 1955–60 both countries had fought alongside the British in the Malayan Emergency, and had since maintained a military presence in Singapore as an additional security measure. Again, in 1963, Anzac troops had deployed to Borneo to fight alongside the British Army against Indonesian forces intent upon destroying the newly independent Federation of Malaysia.

As long ago as the fall of Singapore to the Japanese in 1942 both Australian and New Zealand governments had been forced to rethink their foreign policies. It was seen that the defence of both countries could no longer rest solely on membership of the British Empire and Commonwealth, and joint operations with United States forces in the region in 1942–45 naturally turned Canberra and Wellington towards a wider alliance. The cornerstone of Australian and New Zealand security in South-East Asia became the ANZUS Treaty signed in 1951, by which the three signatories agreed a line of mutual assistance against Communist aggression in the region. It was underwritten by the deployment of a major US presence in SE Asia as an immediate counter to the growing Communist threat.

In 1954 the South East Asian Treaty Organization (SEATO) was founded as a further deterrent to Communist expansion. As NATO represented the unity of free nations opposing the expansion of Russian Communism in Europe, so SEATO would counter Chinese Communism in Asia; and in the same year the withdrawal of the French from North Vietnam and the imminent independence of South Vietnam led the USA to become increasingly involved as the political guarantor and military trainer of that new republic. Under the auspices of both ANZUS and SEATO treaties, Australian and New Zealand forces frequently participated in joint military exercises in the region. By the early 1960s both armies had a long-standing experience and mastery of jungle warfare, a skill which was

Bien Hoa, July 1965: tired but cheerful soldiers of 1RAR after the battalion's first major operation, sitting on their 08/37 Pattern packs. Several items are typical of this early period: note M1956 webbing, metal canteens, and the long three-buckle gaiters and Owen SMG at bottom right. Two types of machete are carried: British – left, with handle wrapped in hessian – and US WWII, right. The British jungle hat is worn in several of the infinite variety of shapes into which it could be moulded.

Many joint infantry/armour operations were carried out in Vietnam; this infantry patrol passes a Centurion of 1 Armd Regt, RAAC in 1970. The lead man wears old style 'jungle greens' (JGs); his belt kit has two large Australian-made M1956 pouches at the front and green-dyed 37 Pattern basic pouches on his hips, and his M16 is camouflage-painted. The 'tankies' wear locally made baseball caps – probably in Armoured Corps black – with the RAAC badge.

For more information on Australian Centurions in Vietnam, see Simon Dunstan's *Vietnam Tracks*, Osprey, 1982 & 2004

soon to be called upon once again.

At the beginning of 1965 South Vietnam, a protocol state of the SEATO treaty and one of the region's most important 'dominos', was about to topple. On 29 April 1965 Australian Prime Minister Robert Menzies declared his government's intention of sending an infantry battalion to Vietnam. He stated his reasons for committing Australian troops as being rooted firmly in the belief that 'the take-over of South Vietnam would pose a direct military threat to Australia and all the countries of South-East Asia'.

New Zealand's first tangible assistance to Vietnam was a small engineer team of two officers and 24 other ranks who arrived in June 1964. Designated the New Zealand Army Detachment Vietnam (NZADVN), the sappers worked in and around the town of Thu Dau Mot on a variety of civil aid projects before being withdrawn to New Zealand in June 1965. Wellington also responded to its ANZUS commitment by contributing an artillery battery to the Anzac force. New Zealand's attitude to the worsening situation in Vietnam to some extent mirrored that of Australia, although her continuing involvement in Borneo meant that the small New Zealand Army was already fully committed to its SEATO role.

ADVISERS

The first Australians to deploy to Vietnam in 1962 were, like the first Americans, military advisers tasked with training the fledgling South Vietnamese Army. The Australian Army Training Team Vietnam (AATTV) – soon abbreviated to 'The Team' – would serve in Vietnam for more than ten years, and would become Australia's longest serving and most decorated unit for its small size. Members of the AATTV were all career officers and senior NCOs, mainly from the infantry, SAS and the Commando companies, with a leavening of signallers, engineers and other specialists. All were hand-picked for the task, being experts in the newly defined art of 'counter-revolutionary warfare' (CRW). Most had served in Malaya, and within the unit was a reservoir of experience and practical knowledge that the Americans were keen to exploit. As well as being an unquestionable military asset, the Team also represented a visible reminder of the spirit of the ANZUS Treaty, and members were encouraged to wear 'Australia' titles on uniform and to fly the Australian flag at their Saigon headquarters.

Initially the Team fitted into the existing US advisory structure, under the central control of the Military Assistance Advisory Group (MAAG) and later Military Assistance Command Vietnam (MACV). It was split between the two training centres of Hiep Khanh and Dong Da in the northern province of Thua Thien. As the Team expanded its members were spread throughout the length and breadth of South Vietnam, although its main focus would remain in the north.

The camp at Hiep Khanh trained members of the Vietnamese Regional Forces, a civil guard organisation tasked with the defence of key installations. The RFs were considered poor relations to the Army of the Republic of Vietnam (ARVN), and were equipped and paid accordingly. The National Training Centre at Dong Da was, by contrast, run by the ARVN and consequently was well funded and equipped. Other Team members were posted to the Duc My Ranger Training Centre, where they instructed Vietnamese Ranger (Biet Dong Quan) students in jungle, swamp and mountain warfare.

Sgt K.A.Edwards instructs *Montagnard* 'strikers' in the Central Highlands. Like the officer at left (identified by a holstered pistol – a mark of status among Vietnamese), Edwards wears the indigenous 'tiger-stripe' camouflage uniform with matching short-brimmed jungle hat. The rank of sergeant was unusual in the AATTV, most members being warrant officers; later in the war an intake of corporals was accepted to boost Team numbers.

Into the field

As the war progressed and the Team grew in numbers its role was broadened, to include advisory duties on combat operations. Early in 1964 a directive that had restricted advisers to their schools and villages was lifted, and Team members began to accompany Vietnamese units in the field. Following the withdrawal of the French the new republic had largely wasted the potential of the small pool of experienced Vietnamese junior leaders created within French Colonial combat units, and rank and responsibility had most often been distributed for reasons of political patronage. By the middle of 1964 it was becoming apparent that the ARVN was still woefully incapable of holding its own against the enemy, and MACV requested more Australian advisers to operate with Vietnamese field units at battalion level. These additional Australians, mostly warrant officers, took the place of American lieutenants in four-man advisory teams. American advisory teams would typically consist of a captain, first lieutenant (or Australian WO), and two specialist sergeants, assisting the Vietnamese battalion in all aspects of field operations, logistics and training, with a special emphasis on the co-ordination of air and artillery support. The Team lost its first member, WO Kevin Conway, when his unit was attacked on 6 July 1964.

In early 1964 the camp at Hiep Khanh was closed and the Team took the opportunity to focus more on the Ranger training centre at Duc My. The Vietnamese Rangers were increasingly seen as one of the few indigenous units capable of facing the enemy in any significant way, and Duc

My was growing in size and importance. The four Australians posted there were from the Special Air Service Regiment. An early success story for the Team was that of Capt Barry Petersen, a Malaya veteran who was given the task of forming paramilitary units from the ethnic minority *Montagnard* tribes of the Central Highlands, whose military potential had always been hampered by the mutual hostility between them and the lowland 'Annamites' of Vietnam. Petersen was singularly successful in this venture, and within two years he had formed an effective force of more than a thousand tribesmen. In true adviser style he was quick to adopt the customs and traditions of the 'Yards', even taking the time to learn their notoriously difficult language. For his efforts he was rewarded with the tribesmen's loyalty and trust, and was even elected as an honorary tribal chieftain. Petersen's force eventually outgrew the concept of simple village defence, and began to undertake successful offensive operations against enemy units in the vicinity. Ultimately their traditional mistrust of the hill tribes led the Saigon authorities to regard Petersen's 'private army' with unease, and the project was terminated.

As the war expanded still further, members of the Team were posted to a wide range of locations and units depending on their individual military specialisations. Team members would typically find themselves serving with one other Australian or American adviser in an otherwise all-Vietnamese unit. AATTV men served in Vietnamese armour, artillery and special forces units as well as in the more usual infantry and Ranger battalions. Appointments could also include duty with the Regional and Popular Forces (RF/PF or 'Ruff-Puffs'), and with the National Field Police Force. Many Team members served with US Special Forces, mainly concentrated along Vietnam's western borders and the associated infiltration routes. Most Australians working with USSF were attached to Mobile Strike Force ('Mike Force') units in I Corps. Others served in the CIA-sponsored Provisional Reconnaissance Units, a secretive programme concerned with identifying and eliminating the Viet Cong infrastructure.

In its final phase the Team was again expanded in 1970 as Australian ground troops began their withdrawal from South Vietnam. As part of the programme of 'Vietnamization' (whose goal was to ensure that the Vietnamese forces were capable of taking over from the departing

Americans and Australians), a jungle warfare training centre was established in Phuoc Tuy province. When the combat units of the Australian Task Force withdrew in 1971, AATTV's role reverted solely to training; all combat advisory duties were suspended, and in December 1972 the Team itself was finally withdrawn and disbanded.

The role of the combat adviser in Vietnam required a unique combination of military skills as well as personal fortitude. With an average age of 35, the Team members were all mature and seasoned soldiers and ideally suited to the task. Over the ten years of AATTV's existence 992 Australians and ten New Zealanders served with this unique unit, with many serving multiple tours. Thirty-three Team members died on active service; and the unit's awards include the US Meritorious Unit Citation, the Vietnamese Cross of Gallantry, 245 individual American and 376 Vietnamese awards.

Victoria Cross awards

Among the 105 Australian decorations awarded to Team members were no fewer than four Victoria Crosses. The first of these was awarded to WO2 Kevin 'Dasher' Wheatley. Wheatley was already a legend in the close-knit Australian Army, having joined AATTV from 1RAR; everyone knew Dasher, 'a rough, wild man and a good soldier'. On 13 November 1965, Wheatley and fellow adviser WO2 Ron Swanton were assigned to a Civilian Irregular Defense Group (CIDG) company on a sweep in the Tra Bong valley. Shortly after leaving their camp the unit came under concentrated fire from a large Viet Cong force. In the initial contact Swanton was hit in the chest, and the CIDG broke and ran. Wheatley dragged and carried the mortally wounded Swanton across 250 yards of exposed rice paddy to the shelter of a treeline. When it became apparent that he could not outrun his pursuers, Wheatley was seen to set Swanton down and turn to face the enemy, a grenade in each hand. The bodies of both Australians were recovered the next day, and Kevin Wheatley was posthumously awarded the Victoria Cross. The circumstances of Wheatley's death quickly spread through the ranks of the newly arrived 1RAR, and cast an unfortunate shadow over the reliability of the South Vietnamese forces in the minds of many Australians.

In May 1969, WO2 R.S.Simpson was commanding a SF Mike Force company on a sweep near the Laotian border. As his lead platoon became engaged by a strong force of enemy – this time North Vietnamese regulars – Simpson led the remainder of the company in a counter-attack. Again, a fellow Team member (WO2 M.Gill) was hit, and Simpson ran across open ground under fire to carry him to safety. With the coming of darkness the situation became untenable, and Simpson ordered the company to break contact, personally covering the withdrawal and carrying a wounded Vietnamese platoon leader. As an adjunct, five days later Simpson was again engaged in a contact with the NVA. With his battalion officer dead and most of his NCOs down, he again displayed remarkable courage and leadership, preventing the enemy from advancing through his position until the wounded had

WO2 Keith Payne VC, September 1969. In May of that year Payne's 212 Coy, 1st Mike Force Bn was attacked by a large enemy force. Although wounded, Payne rallied his unit under intense small arms, RPG and mortar fire, and established a defensive perimeter, which he left four times to recover a wounded US adviser and several other casualties. He then managed to extricate his party of three advisers and some 40 *Montagnard* strikers through enemy-held territory, a feat for which he was awarded the Victoria Cross.
Here he wears the AMF 'Rising Sun' patch lower than usual, above his crown badge of rank. The presentation of the USSF green beret to soldiers of another country was a rare honour; Payne's bears his RAR brass cap badge on the usual 5th SF Group patch.

been evacuated. Simpson placed himself between the enemy and the wounded, including fellow Australian WO2 A.M.Kelly, and almost single-handedly fought off several assaults. Wheatley and Simpson, together with the other Victoria Cross recipients Maj Peter Badcoe and WO2 Keith Payne, typified the calibre of men in AATTV, and exemplified the Australian code of 'mateship' that ultimately led to such acts of self-sacrificing courage.

Bien Hoa, summer 1965: a patrol from 1RAR move out along a perimeter track at the airbase. The lead man has rigged a set of shoulder pads to the straps of his 37 Pattern pack; the AMF 'Rising Sun' patch can just be seen on his left shoulder. The centre man has corporal's stripes apparently on a brassard, and what became a fairly standard set of equipment in 1RAR: basically US M1956, augmented with larger 37/44 Pattern British pouches on the hips.

THE PROFESSIONALS

First deployments, 1965

In late May and early June 1965, the First Battalion, Royal Australian Regiment (1RAR) arrived in South Vietnam as Australia's contribution to the tri-national ANZUS Brigade forming at Bien Hoa airbase near Saigon.[1] The brigade would also include 161 Battery, Royal New Zealand Artillery, and came under the operational command of the US 173rd Airborne Brigade, which provided the other two infantry battalions. The ANZUS Brigade was conceived as a mobile 'fire brigade' force which would keep the enemy off balance during the critical build-up phase in War Zone D around the capital.

1RAR was already Australia's 'Ambrose' Battalion – i.e. it was on stand-by to deploy anywhere in South-East Asia at the request of SEATO. Commanded by LtCol Ivan Brumfield, 1RAR was made up entirely of regular career soldiers; it had just been reconfigured from a 1,500-strong force into a new 'Pentropic' battalion of just 800, made up of five rifle companies. The battalion deployed to Bien Hoa with an accompanying APC Troop, Signal Detachment, and Logistical Support Company. 1RAR was a tightly-knit group of professional soldiers whose previous service gave the unit great cohesion and confidence. The officers, NCOs and men knew each other well and had trained hard for a deployment to South-East Asia; most of the NCO cadre had served with the battalion in Malaya. This initial Australian deployment was undertaken against a background of intense political argument: there was already a growing lobby against the war in Vietnam in general and Australia's involvement in particular. Prime Minister Menzies had also angered many Australians by reintroducing conscription for overseas military service, though no National Servicemen were in fact included in the initial 1RAR group.

1 The Royal Australian Regiment is not a regiment in the traditional sense of a unit comprising a set number of simultaneously existing battalions, but is the overall designation of the Australian Army's infantry arm, within which varying numbers of individual battalions are raised according to need and circumstance.

In mid-July 1965 the ANZUS Brigade at Bien Hoa was augmented by 161 Battery, RNZA. As New Zealand's infantry regiment and Ranger Squadron (NZSAS) were already committed to Borneo, it was felt that a field battery that could provide direct support to 1RAR was a logical alternative. The Papakura-based 161 Bty was, like 1RAR, an all-regular unit with the same integrity and confidence fostered by years of training. The battery arrived with its full establishment of four air-portable 105mm L5 pack howitzers, supported by a logistical detachment. These field pieces were ideally suited to the type of mobile operations that the ANZUS Bde was to conduct. Unlike 1RAR and the subsequent Australian battalions, 161 Bty did not rotate as a unit at the end of its year-long tour. Personnel were replaced on a monthly basis from a trained pool in New Zealand, with approximately 150 officers and men passing through the battery each year. Operationally the New Zealanders had to 'marry-up' with 1RAR and 'tie-in' with the 173rd Airborne. The 'marry-up' proved smooth, since both Australia and New Zealand followed common British Army procedures. The fact that 161 Bty's commanding officer knew his 1RAR counterpart from Duntroon (Australia's Sandhurst or West Point equivalent) also helped, and both had served in the Commonwealth Division in Korea. The 'tie-in' with the Americans also proved surprisingly straightforward, only requiring the New Zealand gunners to change their fire-order procedures to the American system.

Initially the Anzac elements at Bien Hoa were put into a defensive posture, their role being to ensure the security of the important airbase against attack. When 1RAR arrived the US paratroopers of the 173rd were already accommodated in rows of tents which were being replaced by permanent prefabricated huts. By contrast, the Australians were allotted an area of adjacent scrubland and, over the course of the coming weeks, had to build their base from scratch. As the weeks passed the contrast in living arrangements between the Americans and Anzacs was a daily reminder of the different attitudes of the three countries in the tri-national force. The American area grew rapidly to include corrugated iron buildings with concrete floors, mess halls, bars and a PX facility; by night the area was ablaze with light and hummed to the sound of many generators powering air-conditioning units. By comparison the Anzac area remained spartan and businesslike, with all ranks living in tents and not a single light showing during the hours of darkness. Another marked difference was that the Americans employed a large number of Vietnamese civilians as cooks, cleaners and in a variety of

September 1967: Maj Peter White, commanding A Coy, 2RAR (left) briefs a platoon commander, Lt Trevor Lyons. White wears the final version of US tropical combat uniform, with concealed buttons and without shoulder straps. Lyons wears standard JGs and a British hat. He has configured his personal equipment so that the bulk of the load is carried on a US lightweight rucksack frame, with only canteens and (presumably) ammunition pouches on his belt order. Strapped to the frame is an 08/37 Pattern pack, with M1956 canteens attached by cutting slits for their slide-keepers in the sides of the pack. An M1956 'butt pack' is fixed to the bottom of the frame with an additional canteen hung from its side – the length of the frame prevents the butt pack being worn in the usual position on the back of the belt.

other odd-job roles. The Anzacs did not employ civilians, and no Vietnamese nationals were allowed in their area.

When Australian officers and NCOs went out on patrol with the 173rd they quickly learned that the Americans had a very different attitude to patrolling. The paratroopers liked to patrol in strength in a manner that invited contact with 'Charlie'; the Australians favoured a stealthier approach, and would often stay out for much longer periods. For all their differences the young Australians and Americans got on together surprisingly well: the Diggers considered the paratroopers brave enough, if lacking in thorough training, while the Americans were amused by what they regarded as the Australians' excessive caution, while appreciating their professionalism. A growing bond between the three units manifested itself in the traditional trading of personal uniform and equipment. The Americans coveted the Aussies' large ammunition pouches, canvas shower-bucket, two-man plastic 'Hutchie' shelter, and the famous Australian slouch hat. The Diggers for their part sought US rations, tropical combat uniforms and jungle boots. As a further declaration of ANZUS unity the 173rd gave unprecedented authorization for 1RAR to wear its colourful winged bayonet shoulder patch – an offer kindly meant, but tactfully declined by Col Brumfield.

TASK FORCE

1966: 'Take over Phuoc Tuy'

During 1RAR's tour with the ANZUS Bde some 22 major operations were conducted under the administrative and operational control of the 173rd Airborne. Working with the Americans had been largely successful, but was complicated by the different equipment used and the logistical problems this engendered. After 12 months the Australians and their American counterparts were still very different fighting forces: the 173rd were still pursuing a conventional 'big' war, while the Australians continued to fight a counter-insurgency 'patrol' war.

In March 1966 the Australian government approved the formation of an independent Australian Task Force to be known as 1ATF. The formation of 1ATF was the result of political pressure – both from the Americans, who wanted a more substantial Australian presence in Vietnam, and from Canberra, which wanted to regain operational control of its troops in theatre. There

1969: publicity shot of a UH-1D 'Bushranger' gunship of No.9 Sqn RAAF being armed. The XM158 launcher pod for 7x 2.75in rockets, and a pair of M21 'Miniguns', made up the M16 armament system typically fitted to gunship Hueys. Above are 'twin sixties' in their stripped-down aircraft configuration, minus handguards but with added empty case deflectors; the large storage bins held long continuous belts with many hundred rounds of 7.62mm ammunition. On the gunner's seat can be seen an AFH-1 flight helmet and aircrew body armour; an SLR – cut down in SAS fashion and with a 30-rd magazine – is stowed as a personal weapon. Wall bins hold further magazines and smoke grenades. The pilot wears RAAF rank and the RAAF's national title on the shoulder strap of his Australian flying suit.

were a number of sound military considerations for creating a single autonomous military force (to include the New Zealand contingent). Firstly, the logistical supply problems would be vastly eased; secondly and more importantly, there was a desire to allow Australian units the freedom to conduct operations in their own style, consistent with their training and experience. It was felt that an Australian presence strong enough to be independent and identifiable was both politically and militarily necessary. To this end 1ATF was formed with two infantry battalions, an APC squadron, artillery regiment, SAS squadron, and HQ, supply and signal elements – an initial strength of some 4,500 personnel.

Lying south-east of Saigon, Phuoc Tuy Province was approximately 62km east to west and 30km north to south (38 by 18 miles); most of its 103,000 inhabitants were concentrated around the provincial capital of Baria. The countryside around the major towns had been thoroughly infiltrated by the Communist Viet Minh movement during the French Indochina War of 1946–54, and was now largely in Viet Cong hands, with the Saigon government exercising little control over the rural population. The challenge to the Australians was to regain control of the province, and to this end US Gen William Westmoreland instructed 1ATF commander Brig O.D.Jackson to 'Take over Phuoc Tuy'.

The Task Force set up its forward base in the Nui Dat rubber plantation, with its logistical supply base a little further south at Vung Tau (to the Aussies, 'Vungers'). The site chosen at Nui Dat lay on a steep, jungle-covered hillside rising some 60m (200ft) above the surrounding countryside. As well as being located between the main concentrations of enemy and the bulk of the province's civilian population, it also offered the space to build an airfield. The tents and huts that sprang up between the rows of rubber trees were to be the Task Force's home for the next six years.

The enemy in Phuoc Tuy came in two distinct forms, descended from the 'popular' and 'regional' forces of the French war. The first were the locally raised units that were formed by village committees – 'farmers by day, fighters by night', of which the largest was Provisional Mobile Battalion D445, with some 550 men. More formidable were the so-called 'main force' units who operated from bases in the north of the province. At the time of 1ATF's deployment the enemy had two main force regiments in Phuoc Tuy, the 274th and 275th, each of three battalions – a total of around 4,000 men under the operational control of the 5th VC Division HQ. In spring 1966 the enemy clearly had the upper hand in Phuoc Tuy, and the problems of regaining control of the province were manifold; all districts were either under direct Communist rule or were heavily taxed by the VC.

In May 1966 the Fifth Battalion, Royal Australian Regiment (5RAR) landed at Vung Tau and moved to its new home at the Nui Dat

Luscombe Field, Nui Dat, 1967: 2nd Lt Ross Goldspink of 161 Recce Flight points to a patched bullet hole in the bubble of his OH-13 Sioux (called the 'Possum' in Australian service). 161 Flt also operated larger helicopters, and fixed wing aircraft such as the Cessna 0-1 Bird Dog. Most Army pilots wore standard JGs and GP boots; Goldspink displays embroidered, padded pilot wings over his left pocket, and the single 'pip' of his rank on a shoulder slide. The US APH-5 helmet is in its white issue finish; they were often resprayed green. Other typical aircrew items are kid leather gloves, and a personal sidearm worn on the web belt in an old 37 Pattern holster. Note the Australian Army Aviation Corps decal visible just right of the pilot.

One of the best known images of the Australians in Vietnam, Sgt Mike Coleridge's picture was subsequently photo-engraved on to Canberra's Vietnam War Memorial. Taken on 26 August 1967 on the Lang Phuoc Hai/Dat Do road, it shows Diggers being airlifted back to Nui Dat at the end of Operation 'Ulmurra', part of the larger Operation 'Atherton'. Here 5 Ptn, B Coy, 7RAR are being marshalled for pick-up by movements controllers in high-visibility vests. They wear the usual mix of M1956 and 37/44 Pattern webbing; three types of pack are evident – 08/37, US lightweight, and ARVN rucksacks. The metal poles are mine/booby-trap probes.

base; and the arrival of 6RAR in June completed the infantry element of the Task Force. Unlike the First Battalion, both 5RAR and 6RAR contained a high proportion of conscript National Servicemen ('Nashos') in their ranks. A two-year term of compulsory National Service had been re-introduced in November 1964 when it became apparent that the regular volunteer army would be unable to meet the troop levels required for service in Vietnam. In this manner the Royal Australian Regt was increased from its four regular battalions to nine within two years. Initially it was planned that no more that 50 per cent of a unit's strength were to be National Servicemen, but as the war progressed this proportion was necessarily increased. 'Nashos' would eventually make up the bulk of Australia's forces in Vietnam, especially in the infantry battalions, and even the SAS Regt would accept carefully selected volunteers from among National Servicemen into its exclusive ranks.

Like 1RAR at Bien Hoa, the newly arrived members of the Task Force had to build their own base before offensive operations could begin. Areas were cleared and fighting pits dug under the uncomfortable conditions of the monsoon rains; again, accommodation was to be basic, and for the next six years the Anzacs at Nui Dat were not to enjoy the amenities taken for granted by American servicemen at US bases across Vietnam. In the weeks before the Task Force was at full strength the VC continuously probed the base, looking for an opportunity to attack the Australians in force; when 6RAR arrived this opportunity passed, and the anticipated attack never came. With his force complete Brig Jackson began a programme of aggressive patrolling around Nui Dat. Pushing patrols further and further out from the base, the Australians rapidly began to force the Viet Cong from the surrounding countryside; the enemy's monopoly in Phuoc Tuy was over.

CHRONOLOGY

The following is a brief and simplified chronology of some of the more significant operations conducted by Anzac troops, listed under the month when they started, although some lasted more than a month. It also includes the arrival dates of some selected units, under the month when the bulk of the unit arrived in theatre. The Order of Battle (page 16) gives further details.

1962

August	First AATTV personnel arrive in Saigon

1964

June	Detachment of RNZ Engineers deploy to Thu Dau Mot
September	1 SAS Coy RAR is expanded to battalion strength and redesignated 1 SAS Regt (SASR)
November	Australia introduces two-year selective National Service (in US terms, 'the draft')

1965

May	1RAR deploys as part of ANZUS Brigade at Bien Hoa
June	1 APC Troop, RAAC deploys to Bien Hoa
July	161 Battery, RNZ Artillery deploys to Bien Hoa
November	Operation 'Hump'

1966

January	Operation 'Crimp'
February	Operation 'Rolling Stone'
March	Formation of independent Australian Task Force
April	5RAR (first tour); 6RAR (first tour); 3 Sqn SASR (first tour)
July	Operation 'Hobart'
August	Operation 'Holsworthy'. Battle of Long Tan
October	Operation 'Bundaberg'

1967

January	Operation 'Wollongong'
March	2RAR (first tour)
April	7RAR (first tour)
May	First NZ infantry deploy – Victor 1 Coy, 1RNZIR
June	Operation 'Barossa'
July	Operation 'Cairns'

OPPOSITE **April 1968: Tpr Tom Cowburn of C Sqn, 1 Armd Regt shows Pte Ralph Elliott of 1RAR around his Centurion during infantry/tank training. Elliott wears standard JGs with GP boots and a British jungle hat. His belt order nicely illustrates the concurrent use of Australian, US and British items. On the front of the belt are US 1956 'universal' pouches, from one of which hangs a toggle rope. On his hips are green-dyed British 37 Pattern 'basic' pouches; and at the rear is an M1956 butt pack with M1956 canteens attached. His machete and sheath are Australian, replacing earlier types of both US and British origin. It has a square-tipped parkerized blade and a riveted wooden handle; the canvas sheath – which could be worn on the belt by a belt loop, as here, or hung below it by a wire hanger – features a small pouch for a sharpening stone.**

OPPOSITE **April 1970: signaller Pte Jim Blundell of 6RAR carrying the PRC-25 radio typically lashed high on a US rucksack frame. The lower third of the body housed the large dry-cell battery, which had an average life of 20 hours. Part-valve, part-transistor, the '25 set' had some 900 channels and a range of anything between 3 and 5 miles (5–8km), although a weak battery could cut that distance drastically. It was generally reliable if well maintained.**

August	Operation 'Atherton'
December	3RAR (first tour); Whiskey 1 Coy, 1 RNZIR
1968	
January	1RAR (second tour); 4RAR (first tour). Operation 'Coburg'
February	1 & 2 Tps, C Sqn, 1st Armd Regt RAAC bring first Centurion Mk 5/1 tanks to Vietnam
March	First action by Centurions in Operation 'Pinaroo'
April	Operation 'Cooktown Orchid'
May	Operation 'Toan Thang 1', Bien Hoa Province. Battles of FSB Coral and Balmoral – A Sqn 3rd Cav Regt, C Sqn 1st Armd Regt
June	Operation 'Redwing'
July	Operation 'Merino'
August	Operation 'Platypus'
September	Operation 'Hawkesbury'. 3 & 4 Tps complete C Sqn, 1st Armd Regt RAAC
October	Operation 'Stirrup Cup'
November	9RAR; 4 Troop, NZSAS
December	Operation 'Goodwood 1'
1969	
January	5RAR (second tour). Operation 'Goodwood 2'
February	B Sqn relieves C Sqn, 1st Armd Regt
March	Operation 'Twickenham 1'
April	Operation 'Surfside'
May	6RAR (second tour)
June	Operation 'Hammer'. Battle of Binh Ba – 5RAR, B Sqn 3rd Cav Regt, B Sqn 1st Armd Regt
July	Operation 'Waiouru'
August	Operation 'Mundingburra'
September	Operation 'Burnham'
October	Operation 'King's Cross'
November	8RAR (first tour)
1970	
February	7RAR (second tour). Operation 'Hammersley'
March	Operation 'Townsville'
April	2RAR (second tour). Operation 'Nudgee'
May	4RAR (second tour). Operation 'Capricorn'
June	Operation 'Petrie'
October	1 NZATTV deploys to Chi Lang
1971	
February	3RAR (second tour). Operation 'Phoi Hop'
June	Operation 'Bowhani Junction'
August	Operation 'Cudlee Creek'
October	Operation 'Valiant'
November	4RAR returns to Australia
December	1ATF is stood down
1972	
February	2 NZATTV formed at Dong Ba Thin
December	Remaining Australian and New Zealand personnel withdrawn from Vietnam

AUSTRALIAN ARMY ORDER OF BATTLE
SOUTH VIETNAM, 1962–72

Australian Force Vietnam (AFV)
HQ Australian Army Force Vietnam
HQ Army Assistance Group Vietnam
Australian Embassy Guard Platoon
Defence and Employment Platoon
Field Operations Research Section
HQ Australian Force Cash Office
Australian Civil Affairs Unit
Postal Unit

1 Australian Task Force (1ATF)
HQ 1 Australian Task Force
Detachment, 1 Division Cash Office
Detachment, Australian Force Vietnam
  Cash Office
Provost Section, 1 Provost Company
Australian Force Vietnam Provost Unit
1 Australian Reinforcement Unit
Defence & Employment Platoon

**1 Australian Logistic Support Group
(1ALSG)**
Australian Logistic Support Company
HQ 1 Australian Logistic Support Group
2 Detachment, Australian Force Vietnam
  Cash Office
Detachment, 1 Divisional Postal Unit
Detachment, 1 Comm Z Postal Unit
Detachment, 5 ASCO Unit
HQ 2 Australian Force Canteen Unit
Detachment, 2 AFCU
1 Platoon, 2 AFCU
67 Ground Liaison Section
1 Australian Rest & Convalescence Centre
AFV Amenities & Welfare Unit

**Australian Army Training Team Vietnam
(AATTV)**

Royal Australian Armoured Corps
1 APC Troop (June 1965–May 1966)
1 APC Squadron (May 1966–Jan 1967)
A Sqn, 3 Cavalry Regiment (Jan 1967–May 1969)
B Sqn, 3 Cav Regt (May 1969–Jan 1971)
A Sqn, 1 Armoured Regt (Dec 1969–Dec 1970)
B Sqn, 1 Armd Regt (Feb–Dec 1969)
C Sqn, 1 Armd Regt (Feb 1968–Feb 1969,
                & Dec 1970)
Detachment, 1 Forward Delivery Troop

Royal Australian Artillery
105 Field Battery (1965–66)
1 Field Regiment:
101 Field Battery (1966–67, & 1969–70)
103 Field Bty (1966–67)
105 Field Bty (1969–70)
4 Field Regt:
106 Field Bty (1967–68, & 1970–71)
107 Field Bty (1970–71)
108 Field Bty (1967–68)
12 Field Regt:
A Field Bty (1971)
102 Field Bty (1968–69)
104 Field Bty (1968–69, & 1971)
131 Divisional Locating Bty (1966–71)

Royal Australian Engineers
Royal Australian Survey Corps
Royal Australian Signal Corps

Infantry
Royal Australian Regiment
1st Battalion (1RAR) (May 1965–July 1966)
                (Jan 1968–Jan 1969)
2RAR (Mar 1967–June 1968)
      (April 1970–June 1971)
3RAR (Dec 1967–Dec 1968)
      (Feb–Oct 1971)
4RAR (Jan 1968–May 1969)
      (May 1970–Mar 1972)
5RAR (April 1966–July 1967)
      (Jan 1969–Mar 1970)
6RAR (April 1966–July 1967)
      (May 1969–May 1970)
7RAR (April 1967–April 1968)
      (Feb 1970–Mar 1971)
8RAR (Nov 1969–Nov 1970)
9RAR (Nov 1968–Dec 1969)

Special Air Service Regiment
1 Squadron (1967–68, & 1970–71)
2 Sqn (1968–69, & 1971)
3 Sqn (1966–67, & 1969–70)

Australian Army Aviation Corps
161 Reconnaissance Flight (1965–72)

Australian Intelligence Corps
Detachment, 1 Divisional Intelligence Unit
1 Psychological Operations Unit

Royal Australian Army Service Corps
Royal Australian Army Medical Corps
Royal Australian Army Dental Corps
Royal Australian Army Nursing Corps
Royal Australian Army Ordnance Corps
**Royal Australian Electrical &
Mechanical Engineers**

The lead scout of a local patrol (note absence of pack) from Victor Coy leaving the 'Horseshoe' base at Nui Dat; he can just be seen to wear the New Zealanders' black cravat with a white kiwi motif, as do several other men in the original uncropped photo. Shortly after this picture was taken the lead scout became a mine casualty. (NZ Army PR)

NEW ZEALAND INFANTRY

In March 1967 the New Zealand government decided to increase its commitment to Vietnam by deploying an infantry rifle company. Accordingly a reinforced company group, including mortar and assault pioneer sections and designated V Company, Royal New Zealand Infantry Regiment, arrived in May 1967.

V Company (known as 'Victor 1') was placed under the operational command of 1ATF and was attached to the newly arrived 2RAR. In December a further New Zealand company, W Coy ('Whiskey 1'), also deployed and was attached to 2RAR.

In March 1968 a new Anzac link was forged when both Victor and Whiskey companies were merged with 2RAR to form a fully integrated unit designated 2RAR/NZ (ANZAC) Battalion, with an Australian commanding officer and New Zealand second in command. This unique arrangement continued until November 1970, with successive Victor and Whiskey companies being assigned to whichever Australian battalion was in theatre at that time. Because the New Zealand rotation system differed from the Australian, the make-up of the Anzac Bn changed frequently. Its progressive composition was as follows:

2RAR/NZ (ANZAC) Bn (March 1967 to May 1968):
Victor 2 Coy (March 1967–May 1968)
Victor 3 Coy (May 1967–May 1968)
Whiskey 1 Coy (March 1967–May 1968)

4RAR/NZ (ANZAC) Bn (June 1968 to May 1969):
Victor 3 Coy (June 1968–May 1969)
Victor 4 Coy (8–18 May 1969)
Whiskey 1 Coy (June–Nov 1968)
Whiskey 2 Coy (Nov 1968–May 1969)

New Zealand rifleman, circa 1970. Australian tropical JGs and M1956 web gear are typical; less so is the Vietnamese-made jungle hat in 'tiger-stripe' fabric. Uniform regulations were generally adhered to in the NZ rifle companies, and it is unusual to see individuals deviating from the prescribed combat uniform even at this stage of the war. The shell dressing taped to the butt of the SLR was almost universal among Anzac infantry. Note also that the weapon's carrying handle has been removed. (NZ Army PR)

6RAR/NZ (ANZAC) Bn (May 1969 to May 1970):
Victor 4 Coy (May 1969–May 1970)
Victor 5 Coy (8–14 May 1970)
Whiskey 2 Coy (May 1969–Nov 1969)
Whiskey 3 Coy (Nov 1969–May 1970)

2RAR/NZ (ANZAC) Bn (May 1970 to May 1971):
Victor 5 Coy (May 1970–May 1971)
Victor 6 Coy (8–22 May 1971)
Whiskey 3 Coy (May–Nov 1970)

A New Zealand M60 gun team in 1970; both men wear British jungle hats, and the gunner has modified his by cutting back the brim and crushing the crown down inside itself in typical Kiwi fashion. The US M60 replaced the British GPMG for units in Vietnam for reasons of logistic convenience, and was generally well liked by the Kiwis, after some initial concerns – the weapon had to be maintained fastidiously if stoppages were to be avoided. Ammunition was needed in large quantities, and both the No.1 and his No.2 carried as much as possible – often up to 600 rounds each – while further belts were distributed among other members of the section. (NZ Army PR)

The New Zealanders who served with the ANZAC Battalions were drawn from the First Battalion, Royal New Zealand Infantry Regiment (1RNZIR), based at Terendak Camp in Malaysia. Unlike Australia, New Zealand never introduced compulsory National Service and her forces were entirely composed of regular volunteer soldiers. Like the pre-conscription Australian Army, 1RNZIR was the epitome of a small, highly motivated professional fighting force – moreover, one that was specially trained to fight in a jungle environment. 1RNZIR had recently served in Borneo and Malaysia, and later companies would still have a cadre of men with such experience to draw upon. Many of the New Zealanders were of Maori extraction, tough natural soldiers with an innate understanding of bushcraft and a fine tradition of infantry soldiering. Though both Australians and New Zealanders employed basically the same operating principles, it became apparent that 1RNZIR's methods as practised in Malaysia differed from those employed by the Australians in Vietnam. A period of adjustment saw these differences ironed out, and in general the two armies integrated seamlessly.

Victor 1 deployed straight from Singapore where it had been attached to the 28th Commonwealth Brigade, and thus had been linked in to the British supply system. Upon arrival in Vietnam the New Zealanders were incorporated into the Australian logistical system in order to standardize equipment within the ranks of the Task Force. Some items, such as individual weapons and mortars, were issued and accounted for by New Zealand; others, such as radios, night vision equipment and rations, were pooled by the ANZAC Battalions as a whole. (It is worth noting that Australia and New Zealand had a 'capitation' arrangement with the United States. Much of the Task Force's equipment was of American origin, from helicopters and APCs to ammunition and rations. Every item was paid for by Canberra and Wellington – as was every American artillery round fired or bomb dropped at the request of 1ATF.)

The New Zealanders in Vietnam represented a uniquely professional asset even within the highly competent environment of the Task Force. Working relations with the Australians were typified by friendly rivalry based on a shared British Army heritage, although the Kiwis had to strive constantly to maintain their national identity in the face of the much larger Australian presence. In general the New Zealanders considered that they stood alone as the only truly professional army in theatre – they would happily work with the Australians at a push, had little regard for the American conscript army, and saw most ARVN units as untrained militia. Close to 4,000 New Zealanders served with the Task Force during the war, the majority within the infantry companies of the ANZAC Battalions; 37 were killed on active service.

THE ANZAC WAY

Operational doctrine

The initial secondment of 1RAR to the US 173rd Airborne Bde had quickly shown up the differences in operating procedure followed by the two allies. The young paratroopers and Diggers were each confirming the military adage that armies will fight a new war in the same way that they fought the closing stages of the last. In simplified terms, the Americans tried initially to fight the war in Vietnam as a Korean War with the addition of helicopters; the Australians fought in the same way as they had in Malaya in the 1950s–60s. Neither method was entirely suited to the unique and evolving situation in Vietnam, and a certain amount of fast learning was required on both parts and at all levels.

The first forays of the ANZUS Bde in War Zone D in 1965 highlighted these fundamental differences in both training and operational thinking. The Americans took to the field in large, noisy units, deliberately looking for contact and relying on tactical mobility and overwhelming fire support. They were sending out a clear message to the enemy: 'Here we are; take us on, and pay the price'. The Australians, on the other hand, patrolled silently and cautiously, dispersing their forces over much wider areas. Their message to the enemy was 'You will never know where we are, but we will find you'.

December 1965: Cpl Lex McAuley of 1RAR leads an old man by the hand after his village has been checked for Viet Cong. McAuley was one of the battalion's Vietnamese linguists; post-war he was the author of several of the most important books about Australia's Vietnam experience. Here he wears sweat-soaked JGs with an extravagantly long 'sweat scarf'. Some men armed with M16s would wear one M1956 and one 37/44 Pattern pouch; note also the toggle rope, and 44 Pattern water bottle carrier. The fixed bayonet was probably for prodding the straw walls of huts for concealed weapons. The man to McAuley's right wears a US tropical combat coat over JG trousers, and WWII US jungle boots of tan leather and green canvas with a built-in buckled gaiter.

With the dissolution of the ANZUS Bde and the formation of 1ATF the two armies went their separate ways, and continued to fight the war each in their own manner; their brief association had been a microcosm of how the war would be fought over the next decade. The Americans would continue to fight a conventional 'big' war, and the Australians a counter-insurgency 'patrol' war. The commanding officer of the US 2/203rd Parachute Infantry Regt of the 173rd Abn Bde recognized the differences in 1965: 'When we [the Americans] found something, we shot at it; we did not wait, establish the patterns, look for opportunities after out-thinking the local VC commander. We were just not patient enough – there was too much to do in too little time. We did not use reconnaissance enough. Our ambushes were there for security, not to kill. The Australians were quiet hunters – patient, thorough, trying to out-think the Viet Cong. I would not have liked to operate at night and know there was a chance of ending up in an Aussie ambush.'

Tactics

Australian small unit tactics had evolved from the Malayan experience and were firmly based on the two basic infantry skills of ambushing and patrolling. Adherence to these fundamentals was the key to Anzac operational procedure, and both Australian and New Zealand infantry were highly trained in these basic arts. A commonly held view among the Anzacs at Nui Dat was that while their American counterparts were certainly not lacking in courage, many of their units simply did not have sufficient grounding in the basic military skills, and placed too great a dependence on technological support. This is obviously a generalisation, but it reflects the Anzac's particular pride in the mastery of his profession.

As the war increased in scope and tempo, however, the Australians and New Zealanders learned to adapt their operating procedures to incorporate the full range of technological advances being introduced by their American allies, especially with regard to air support. Nevertheless, the bread-and-butter work of the infantry companies would remain that of patrolling, and it was in this field that the Anzacs excelled.

In Anzac doctrine patrolling was considered an offensive strategy, and was to be the Task Force's principal method of dominating the countryside around its Nui Dat base and eventually driving the enemy from the province. Thorough and aggressive patrolling kept the enemy on his guard and allowed the Anzacs a sense that they were regaining control of the countryside. American units often felt wary when they ventured outside their huge firebases into what they called 'Indian country', where the VC lurked with impunity; but as one Australian officer put it, 'Under our system, *we* do the lurking.'

An infantry section would be made up of the following elements, in order:
(1) Scout group – usually two men armed with M16s, the forward scouts (in US terms, 'point men') worked in tandem, alternately advancing and covering each other's movements, a short distance ahead of the main body of the patrol. The New Zealanders tended to have specialist full-time scouts, while the Australians rotated the job between the patrol's members. (2) Command group – the patrol commander and his signaller, also both armed with M16s. (3) Gun group – the machine gun group consisted of the two-man M60 gun team and the section second in command. (4) Rifle group – approximately five riflemen armed with SLRs, and one man with a 40mm M79 grenade launcher.

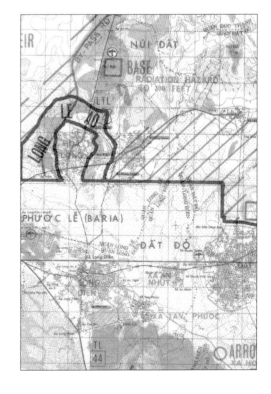

OPPOSITE **Long Khanh, early 1970: Sgt Peter Buckney of 8RAR moves through dense jungle. As a section commander he is armed with an M16, but no rank badges are worn in the field. Buckney carries a visibly back-breaking load. Webbing is Australian M1956, with a compass/dressing case attached to the large ammunition pouch; the British 44 Pattern carrier holds a plastic one-quart canteen. The popular US light-weight rucksack is worn as issued, with the nylon bag low on the frame; an M1956 'bum pack' is secured to the upper frame with several items externally attached. A two-quart collapsible water bladder hangs behind, and a combination entrenching tool in its Australian-made cover at the near side, above a second Australian M1956 canteen.**

A platoon-strength patrol would be made up of three sections each led by a lance-corporal or corporal, the platoon being commanded by a lieutenant. The sections would be dispersed in a variety of formations – single file, one- or two-up, and diamond – all individuals remaining at least five yards apart. The patrol moved as quietly as possible; talking was kept to a minimum and orders were communicated with hand signals. The emphasis was on stealth and concealment, sometimes resulting in painfully slow progress; smoking was only allowed when tactically permissible, and never during the hours of darkness.

At the Jungle Warfare Centre at Canungra the Australian infantryman had learned the art of moving silently through dense bush. He was taught to point his weapon downward at all times so as not to present an obvious outline. As a matter of course rank or other insignia were rarely worn on patrol. In Vietnam both Australian and New Zealand units retained the British practice of 'standing-to' at first and last light. Before last light a patrol base was established, with clearing patrols sent out to sweep the surrounding area. Shallow sleeping/fighting pits known as 'scrapes' were dug, and 'hutchies' or 'bashas' put up. Machine guns and Claymores (command-detonated mines) were set up to cover likely avenues of approach, and sentries were posted. Anzac riflemen were trained to operate in pairs in the field, and weapons and webbing were required to be at hand at all times. During 'stand-to' the entire patrol was on a full state of alert and in their pits with loaded weapons in case the enemy should take advantage of the half-light of dawn or dusk to mount an attack on the position. Australian patrols were typically of longer duration than those undertaken by American infantry units, generally lasting up to several days. It was Australian policy to try to conceal the patrol's location and route for as long as possible, and for this reason helicopter resupply flights were kept to an absolute minimum.

OPPOSITE **Section of 1:100,000 scale map, December 1967, showing an area around the 1ATF base at Nui Dat, Phuoc Tuy province. The diagonally striped areas are marked 'Civilian access permitted 0600–1900 hours'.**

LONG TAN

1ATF's best-known action

The events of this encounter in August 1966 have been well documented, but are worth summarizing here briefly; few other engagements would demonstrate so conclusively the overwhelming effectiveness of Anzac small unit tactics.

In the early hours of 14 August the Task Force base at Nui Dat came under a barrage of recoilless rifle and mortar fire; this was feared to be a prelude to the major attack that had been anticipated for many weeks. One Australian was killed and a further 23 wounded, but the follow-up assault did not materialize. Patrols were sent out from the base to locate the enemy firing positions, but nothing was found.

The patrols continued; and on the 18th, D Company of 6RAR found themselves 'jungle-bashing' towards the Long Tan rubber plantation to the east of Nui Dat. The 108 men of the three rifle platoons could clearly hear the rock music of an Australian concert party back at the base, and most were more concerned with missing the charms of Little Patty McGrath than with any thought of finding the Viet Cong. D Company entered the gloom of the rubber plantation and advanced cautiously, sweating heavily in the late afternoon monsoon heat; the sky was black with imminent rain and the light was rapidly failing. At 16.08 the silence was shattered as enemy in the jungle to the front and sides opened up with intense small arms fire: D Company had been sucked into an ambush.

After the shock of the initial contact, in which two men were killed, the Australians' training took hold and the three platoons went to ground and began to return fire. Eleven Platoon under Lt Gordon Sharp, a National Service officer, was getting the worst of it, and called for artillery support from the New Zealand 105mm battery at Nui Dat. The enemy seemed to be concentrating their efforts on Eleven Platoon, and were seen to be working around the flanks in an attempt to surround them. As Eleven Platoon fought for survival an effort was made by Ten Platoon to relieve them, but this was repulsed by the Viet Cong.

At about this time the monsoon rain began to fall in torrents, and visibility was reduced to about 50 yards in the gloom of the rubber plantation. As 105mm shells from the

Long Hai hills, July 1968: during Operation 'Blue Mountains', Pte Ron Boyd, a machine gunner from 1RAR, prepares a 'brew' using the Hexamine solid fuel cooker. Boyd wears tropical JGs; his green-dyed 'emergency issue' 08/37 pack – apparently padded internally with cardboard from a bulk supply cigarette box – has M1956 canteens attached. Despite its weight of 23lbs (10.5kg) he typically carries his M60 without a sling, with a short belt of link loaded into the feed tray, and a field dressing taped to the bipod. Note that the other belts are carefully protected from contact with the ground; dirty ammunition invariably led to stoppages. In some NZ companies it was standard practice to fire off all unexpended MG ammunition at the end of an operation.

base crashed into the enemy positions, Eleven Platoon desperately tried to break contact; when Lt Sharp was killed his platoon sergeant took over, and the Diggers fought on. By now Maj Harry Smith realized that D Company was in danger of being completely surrounded by an enemy force of battalion, possibly even regimental strength. By 18.30 hours Ten and Twelve Platoons had managed to form a combined position, rapidly digging themselves 12in 'shell scrapes' to provide minimal protection; from within this perimeter Maj Smith co-ordinated the fire of the New Zealand artillery, which was joined by American 155mm pieces. Throughout the battle the New Zealand gunners 'walked' their shells continuously among the VC positions, often only a matter of yards from D Company. Although they fired hundreds of rounds on Smith's instructions, only one Australian was wounded by the artillery fire – a stunning testimony to the skill of the New Zealand gunners.

The surviving Diggers of D Company lay under the blinding rain and calmly returned fire as they had been trained; one young 'Nasho' was heard to chant, 'Up, aim, hold, fire, reload', as he had been taught on the ranges at Pukapunyal. As full darkness fell at around 19.00 the Viet Cong intensified their attacks, and D Company's situation became critical as their ammunition supplies dwindled. The enemy launched repeated 'human-wave' assaults, and it seemed that the Australians must surely be overrun, when a reaction force of 3 Troop, 1 APC Squadron and infantrymen of A Company crashed through the rubber trees from the east, routing two VC companies forming up for another assault. In the face of this counter-attack the enemy disengaged and withdrew.

As daylight broke on the morning of 19 August the full extent of the enemy's defeat became apparent. The Australians counted 245 bodies among the shattered trees, and many more would have been dragged away by their comrades, as was the invariable Viet Cong practice. It was later established by questioning prisoners that the 108 all ranks of D Company had been facing the VC main force 275th Regiment as well as elements of D445 Battalion. The Australians' training in small unit tactics, and a thorough understanding of the use of artillery support, had enabled a single Australian rifle company to hold their own against a force of close to 2,500 of the enemy. Australian casualties of the battle were 18 killed and 21 wounded, mostly from D Company, 6RAR.

SAS

The ultimate exponents of the art of silent patrolling were the Australian and New Zealand Special Air Service (SAS) squadrons. These specialists were unquestionably among the finest professional soldiers in theatre, and their mastery of jungle warfare was absolute. The Australian 3 Squadron was deployed to Nui Dat in June 1966; subsequent squadrons would serve consecutive (often overlapping) tours until the final withdrawal in 1971. SASR established its base on 'SAS Hill' at Nui Dat, where security was tight and visitors to the squadron's lines were discouraged. In October 1968 the 26-man 4 Troop, NZSAS arrived and was operationally attached to the Australian 2 Squadron; thereafter the New Zealand Troop was attached to the resident Australian squadron.

A trooper of 2 Sqn SASR on patrol in 1971, photographed by fellow patrol member Don Barnby. The headband, face paint and ERDL camouflage uniform are all typically SAS; the special patrol gloves were modelled after the US Nomex pilot's gloves worn by many SF and LRRP personnel. On his belt are the special SAS-designed pouches for SLR magazines, with a simple belt loop arrangement allowing them to hang in either of two positions. They took the 20-rd magazine used here, but not the 30-rd magazine, for which 37/44 Pattern pouches had to be employed. The US nylon tropical rucksack with integral steel X-frame, introduced late in 1968, was closely based on the ARVN rucksack, though larger. Both ARVN ('Ranger') and tropical rucksacks had side attachments for canteens.

The SAS role in Vietnam was primarily that of reconnaissance; they were in effect the eyes and ears of the Task Force. The squadrons developed what they called 'recce-ambush patrols' which could last an average of ten days. The nucleus of SAS operations in Vietnam would be the five-man patrol, a break with the traditional SAS four-man patrol; the fifth member was added to provide additional carrying power for the increased amount of ammunition and communications gear dictated by the Vietnam environment.

The ten-day patrol was in fact considered short by SAS standards, since patrols in Malaya had been measured in weeks. This reduction in patrol length was due to the scarcity of drinking water sources within the Australian area of operations, so most supplies had to be carried. A typical recce-ambush patrol was inserted by helicopter and would spend the days before extraction covertly gathering data on enemy dispositions and movement. An ambush would only be attempted at the conclusion of the patrol, and then only if practical; it was always a secondary goal to that of intelligence-gathering.

However, if an unavoidable contact was made the SAS team could deliver an astonishing amount of firepower for its size. SAS contact drills called for immediate and decisive offensive action when a patrol was compromised; many SAS weapons were modified to exaggerate 'muzzle signature' in order to daze and confuse the enemy. The patrol typically carried as much ammunition as a regular infantry section, and while many recce-ambush patrols returned to SAS Hill without having fired a single round, others culminated in swift and ferocious contacts.

The art of camouflage was taken to extremes on SAS patrols. Camouflage clothing was worn as a matter of course, the American ERDL Tropical Combat Uniform being bulk-purchased shortly after its

Trooper Don Barnby of F Troop, 2 Sqn SASR pictured before a patrol in April 1971. He wears standard ERDL camouflage uniform and US jungle boots; the matching jungle hat (either a personal purchase, or bought with squadron funds) has a cut-down brim and cord chinstrap. His belt kit is M1956 with an added pair of SAS M16 pouches worn low on the hips, and a compass case in front. The unique shoulder rig for XM148 grenade rounds is described under Plate F2. The small canisters below the left side pockets are 'mini smoke grenades'.

introduction. The use of camouflage grease-paint on hands and face was universal and thoroughly applied. Weapons were liberally daubed with paint to reduce shine and break up the distinctive outline; even individual magazines were painted. The SAS man's belt kit and pack were also heavily personalized and camouflage-painted. A 2 Squadron file of 1971 directs that 'Patrol members are to cease shaving on the day before insertion'; a further note states that 'All patrol members are to shave within one hour of returning to Nui Dat'. The following are excerpts from the same 2 Sqn patrol brief from 1971:

'*Equipment carried by each patrol member:*
a. Weapon and ammunition as ordered (to include at least two XM148/203 and two L1A1 SLR per patrol)
b. Compass and map
c. Emergency/survival pack
d. Shell dressing
e. Emergency smoke containers × two
f. Water containers
The following will always be carried in the belt or pocket and not in the pack:
1. UHF radio (secured by cord)
2. Individual sheath type knife
3. Shell dressings
4. Ammunition (except Claymores)
5. Smoke grenades
Ammunition: The following is the minimum scale that will be carried per person:
1. 7.62mm – 160 [rounds]
2. 5.56mm – 200
3. 40mm HE and canister – 10
4. 40mm purple – 2 [smoke]
The following grenades will be carried (minimum):
a. 5 × red smoke (per patrol)
b. 5 × yellow smoke (per patrol)
c. 1 × M34/M67 (per person)'

A captured Viet Cong intelligence document provides a candid insight into the enemy's assessment of their Australian adversaries in Phuoc Tuy Province: 'While the *Uc Dai Loi* [Australians] are arrogant and bellicose they are hardy and react fiercely to attack. The Australian patrols and their Ranger tactics are now a serious problem for our Fifth Division… . We cannot maintain a people's war while the Australians remain; the Australians must be eliminated.'

AUSTRALIAN UNIFORMS

The Australian Army that entered Vietnam in 1965 was in a transitional state, moving away from the old ties with Great Britain and beginning to forge new links with the United States. Traditionally the Australian military had followed British Army practices, and its uniforms, insignia,

Bien Hoa, July 1965: Sgt Mervyn Kirby (left) and Pte John Priestly wearing early 'standard JGs' and carrying a combination of generally unsatisfactory gear typical of 1RAR's early operations. Kirby wears a British jungle hat, mangled into a strange shape; Priestly has what seems to be an entirely non-regulation lightweight beret of some kind. Both wear WWII 'Boots, Tropical Stud' with blackened web gaiters, and 37 Pattern basic pouches fitted high on the belt in regulation manner. The tops sagged forward if not buckled to the pack straps, so soldiers tended to slit the rear surface to allow them to be worn low on the belt independently of the pack. Priestly carries an American PRC-10 FM radio, soon to be replaced with the more reliable PRC-25.

weapons and equipment all reflected that influence. A decade of Australian involvement in Vietnam would see Australian field gear evolve from these initial models, through a period of dependence on American design, to its final, entirely Australian-designed and produced state. In 1965 the soldiers of 1RAR went on patrol using very little that was Australian in origin; by 1970 those who followed them would be using very little that was not

However, the periods of British, American and Australian issue overlapped over periods of years, and different patterns were for the most part in use concurrently. The piecemeal distribution of items from such diverse sources meant that most Diggers were issued items from all three. Added to this was the Australian's relaxed approach to personal equipment; the individual soldier had far more say in constructing his set of gear than did his American counterpart. Though his equipment may have been somewhat eclectic, however, the Anzac soldier was always mindful of maintaining a soldierly appearance. Australians and New Zealanders did not follow the American adoption of the 'hippy' culture in the late 1960s, and the proliferation of beads, 'peace signs' and other emblems of an anti-war sentiment that flourished within the American ranks was not mirrored in the Task Force. The Australian Army has traditionally been intolerant of such anti-establishment displays, and for the most part the young conscripts, whatever their views on the war or level of political consciousness, seemed to accept this.

Even the most reluctant 'Nasho' took a pride in the Anzacs' professional reputation, and the wearing of unnecessary adornments on field uniform was considered a tactical mistake if nothing else. Even officially sanctioned insignia, such as badges of rank, were rarely worn on field uniforms – within the close-knit Task Force units everyone knew everyone else. One exception was that a coloured hat band would occasionally be worn as a 'friend or foe' identification aid; this practice had begun in Malaya and was continued in Vietnam, where main force VC and NVA were often dressed in green uniforms and jungle hats very similar to the Australian issue.

'Greens'

The majority of Australian and New Zealand soldiers fought their war wearing a set of jungle-green cotton utilities most commonly referred to simply as 'greens' or 'JGs'. There were two distinct uniforms during the period, the most widely seen being the standard pattern adopted in 1958 as working and combat dress for all arms. The standard JG shirt and trousers were made from 9oz per square inch cotton twill. The shirt buttoned down the full length, with two patch pockets and shoulder straps; the trousers featured an ungainly waist buckle arrangement, and a large map pocket on the left thigh patterned after the WWII British jungle trousers. After Australia's commitment to Vietnam it was considered that a purpose-designed tropical combat uniform was urgently required.

The 'Coat/ Trousers, Mens, Twill Green, Field Combat, Tropical' were field-trialled in Vietnam in August 1966. The then-resident battalion, 5RAR, were issued with 1,500 sets, and reported favourably on the new uniform. The new Tropical Combat Dress – known as 'combat greens' or 'tropical greens' – was made from a 5.5oz cotton twill, and was loosely based on the design of the US Tropical Combat Uniform. The main features apart from the lighter weight of fabric was that the shirt was cut to be worn loose outside the trousers; it had slanted chest pockets that were more accessible while wearing webbing equipment, and pockets for field dressings located at first on the right and later on both sleeves. The trousers did away with the complicated double-buckle arrangement and had a simple fly front, two pockets set on the thighs, and elasticated cuffs.

Christened by the Diggers 'pixie greens' or 'Twiggy greens' (the latter after the famously thin British model girl of the period), this uniform was in fact a poor compromise. Many felt that Australia should simply have purchased the American tropical combat uniform which was already well proven, and popular with anyone who could get hold of a set. Oddly, the new uniform was cut less generously than the old 'standard greens', especially the trousers – hence the nicknames; and though issued in numbers from 1967 onward the tropical JGs would never entirely supersede the old type.

Headgear was a matching green jungle or bush hat (called a 'giggle-hat' by the Australians). Initially these were of British manufacture, with large mesh air holes; from 1968 Australian firms produced their own version, which was virtually identical except for smaller ventilators. Both types featured foliage loops, rarely used for that purpose but occasionally securing strips of coloured cloth as a simple quick-recognition field sign.

M1 steel helmets of both US and Australian manufacture were worn on occasion, usually in conjunction with US-made armour vests. Body armour was typically worn by infantry or APC crews when the

April 1968: Sgt Robert Milwood (left) and Pte Jan Dewonkowski of C Coy 2RAR, at a temporary fire support base in the Long Hai hills during Operation 'Cooktown Orchid'. Milwood has acquired a full set of US Tropical Combat Uniform, which was popular with any Digger who could lay hands on it; his M1956 belt is worn without suspenders, and with a pair of khaki 37 Pattern pouches rigged to hang low. His Australian 'sweat scarf' shows the characteristic oval pattern weave.

mine threat was considered greater than usual. The steel helmet was generally worn with a netting cover, either of WWII vintage or one fashioned from Australian sweat scarf material. Australian-made M1 helmets were identical to the US originals and can be identified only by the distinct blue-green shade of webbing used for the internal fittings, and the various manufacturers' marks.

Berets were worn by some Australian units (see colour plates), most notably by armour, aviation and artillery personnel, as well as by the Royal New Zealand Infantry Regiment companies. The 'Hat, Khaki Felt' – the famous Australian slouch hat – was rarely worn in Vietnam; some Training Team members wore it as a recognition feature, and the RAR battalions wore theirs in transit in and out of theatre.

The Australian combat **footwear** for most of the Vietnam era was the Boot, General Purpose (GP), trialled in 1965 and accepted shortly afterwards. 1RAR had arrived wearing WWII Boots AB or Boots AB/TS (Tropical Studded), worn with high canvas gaiters; both were replaced within the year by the GP boot. The first calf-length combat boots to enter Australian service, they featured a direct-moulded rubber sole and an integral anti-*punji* stick insole of stainless steel. The boot was manufactured to a high quality and gained instant approval; contrary to some sources, it was not made from kangaroo leather but from the more usual cowhide (the kangaroo connection can most likely be traced back to some Digger's sense of humour being taken seriously).

Other footwear occasionally seen were the old full-length British jungle boots in green canvas with rubber soles and ankle reinforcement. These were issued from stocks held in Malaya, but became unpopular in Vietnam as injuries due to *punji* traps increased. An Australian jungle boot was trialled in 1966 but was never widely adopted, as the newly introduced GP boot was found to be superior. These Australian 'Boots, Combat, Wet Weather/Area' were an ankle-length version of the longer British canvas and rubber type. Both British and Australian jungle boots would eventually be relegated to base areas, where they were worn while GP boots were drying out between operations.

The most sought-after footwear among Australians were undoubtedly the US Tropical Combat Boots. These excellent boots were in demand from the outset and were the subject of much ingenious 'reissue' to Australians through various channels. SASR received the American 'J-Boots' as issue from 1966, and held them in high regard. A 3 Squadron signal dated 23 July 1969 and on file at the Australian War Memorial states that 'AHQ has given approval for the issue of

November 1971: Lt Mick Murphy of Tracker Ptn, Support Coy 4RAR checks weapons clear at the end of a patrol. The Diggers wear both standard and later tropical JGs, or a mixture of the two types. Most webbing is Australian M1956, although the central man has a pair of enlarged Australian WWII 'jungle' or 'Bren' pouches. Most of these men have the Australian 'large pack' with canteens, water bladders, etc, attached externally, though the NCO at right has an ARVN rucksack. Field dressings are taped to all weapons. The bipod attached to the centre man's SLR, issued for the M16 but rarely seen in either US or Anzac use, was of light alloy construction with a spring clamp. There was also an 'AR' (automatic rifle) L2A1 version of the SLR, which had a heavier barrel for sustained fire and a handguard that converted to a bipod. In the background, the M113A1 APCs of 3rd Cav Regt RAAC are fitted with Cadillac-Gage T50 machine gun cupolas to protect the commanders.

subject boots (US) to 3 SAS on the basis of 2 pairs per man. The US boot is to be issued on a special-to-theatre basis to SAS only and are not to accompany SAS members on return to Australia'.

The other item of dress synonymous with Australians in Vietnam was the ubiquitous **sweat scarf**. Called either a 'scrim scarf' or 'sweatrag', this was unique to the Australian and New Zealand field uniform, and was a much prized item for trading purposes. The netting came on a large roll and was simply hacked off by the individual, resulting in lengths of anything from 3 to 9 feet. Older styles of British netting were occasionally seen, but the most common was the Australian-made type, which had a distinctive oval pattern.

AUSTRALIAN 'WEBBING'

The Anzac soldier, like his British counterpart, refers to the collection of belts, straps and pouches hung about his person as his 'webbing'. The Anzac in Vietnam was equipped from a variety of sources and served in a period when old patterns were being rethought and superseded by new. The introduction of the 7.62mm Self Loading Rifle into Australian service created one set of requirements, and the issue in Vietnam of several American infantry weapons, notably the M16 rifle, further complicated the picture.[2]

US M1956

The US M1956 individual load carrying equipment (ILCE) had been under consideration for Australian adoption, and was trialled by 1RAR in Malaya during 1961. The commitment of Australian troops to Vietnam decided the question, and the US equipment was accepted so as to simplify resupply procedures.

The set was issued to Australians in three phases. The first was man-ufactured by US suppliers, and was identical to that issued to American troops other than the external markings: in place of the 'US' inkstamp most items bore the Australian Defence Department's initials 'DD' and British-style 'Ordnance arrow'. This initial contract was limited, and 'DD'-marked items were short lived; as demand outstripped supply even this concession to Australian national identity was dropped, and

2 See also MAA 108, *British Infantry Equipments 1908–2000*, and MAA 205, *US Army Combat Equipments 1910–88*

subsequent batches were delivered complete with their 'US' markings. (One 7RAR veteran recalls how some Diggers took umbrage at this, and applied the letters 'A' and 'T' either side of the 'US'.) There was also a third issue of M1956 that was made under contract in Australia. These items were marked with neither 'US' nor 'DD', and though identical in manufacture can be recognized by the distinctive bluish-green shade of some of the webbing. The US-made and 'US'-stamped equipment was by far the most commonly seen version in Australian service, although all three were eventually worn concurrently.

Australian Modified M1956

Although the US set was well received, certain inadequacies soon became apparent in Vietnam. The most obvious anomaly was that the majority of Australians were still armed with the 7.62mm SLR, while the M1956 'universal' ammunition pouch could only accommodate two of the SLR's large 20-round box magazines at a tight squeeze. A new Australian-made pouch was introduced in 1968. The 'Pouch, Ammunition, Large 8¼in x 4in x 3in Deep, Olive Drab' was in essence a bigger version of the standard universal pouch, complete with all the features of the smaller pattern. It was initially constructed of the same dark green cotton duck as the originals, but later runs were made in a distinctive light green canvas with a green nylon edging which was unique to Australian M1956 equipment.

An Australian copy of the one-quart plastic canteen had been produced since 1965, one of the first items of the equipment to be manufactured under licence. The Australian-made canteen ('water bottle' in Australian terminology) was an exact copy but in dark green rather than the brownish olive of the US version; even the heat warning of the original was moulded onto the front.

An Australian-modified canteen cover was introduced in 1968, again a redesign of the original with modifications to the rear. The Australian-made covers retained the US style 'slide-keeper' clips to fit the cover to the belt, but added a wire belt hanger to allow the canteen to be hung from the eyelets in the belt in the same way as the old 44 Pattern covers. Early Australian covers were of cotton duck, but later runs were again of the distinctive light green canvas; both had green-finished snaps instead of the US black snaps.

The entrenching tool carrier was redesigned for Australian use principally by omitting the scabbard fitting designed to take the M14 bayonet, for which Australians had no use. The cover was made in the distinctive light green canvas, with two US-style

Representative early set of equipment, c1965/66; most components are US-made M1956 bulk purchased by Australia. The 'universal' pouches are the early type with stiffened fronts and an eyelet in the pull-tab, though the later type without these features were just as common; note 9ft toggle rope attached to one of them. On the hips are a pair of British 37 Pattern 'basic' pouches (actually Canadian-made, as were many), slit to hang lower; these are dyed 'emergency green', but khaki examples were also used. The green-dyed British-style 08/37 pack has the US-made or Australian-made combination entrenching tool secured in the usual way. It sits above the original small size M1956 combat field pack ('bum pack', to the Diggers); the slightly larger M1961 version was less common. The canteens are of metal M1910 type with black plastic caps. (Private collection)

slide-keepers on the rear and a green snap on the flap. The tool itself was an exact copy of the M1961 Combination Entrenching Tool, in essence a folding shovel with an integral pick-blade and a wooden helve. A separate frog was designed for the SLR's L1A1 bayonet, basically a 37 Pattern frog manufactured in green webbing and with the addition of a wire hanger on the rear as well as the belt loop. Older frogs, mainly 37 Patterns that had been blackened for parade use, were also widely issued with the M1956 equipment.

The field dressing/compass pouch was copied in 1965; quite why this was one of the first items to be made under contract in Australia is unexplained, since the Australian version is identical to the original. Later runs were made from the lighter canvas fabric and had the immediately recognisable green nylon edging and green snap.

The Combat Field Pack or 'butt-pack' was made under contract from 1968, and was in essence a direct copy of the US M1961 version (the M1961 itself being a modified M1956 butt-pack, made larger and with an expanding rubberized 'throat'). Again the Australian version – called a 'bum-pack' by the Diggers – is externally identical to the US original save for the green nylon edging and Ordnance arrow marking.

The belt, suspenders or H-harness, and sleeping gear carrying straps of the M1956 set were all eventually made in Australia, identical to the originals. It is only the markings on many items of M1956 that betray their country of origin, Australian items generally being inkstamped with the Ordnance arrow, and often having this additionally stamped into some metal fittings.

Although Australia was never a member of NATO she did adopt the NATO codification system for military equipment, and was allocated the country identification code '66'. Items of Australian-made M1956 are marked with NATO Stock Numbers (NSN): for example, 8465–66–063–9664 is the Cover, Water Canteen – the first four digits identifying the general class (in this case Personal Equipment), the second pair the country, and the last seven the individual item. It should be emphasized that Australian-production M1956 was never introduced into service as a complete set of equipment. Individual items were redesigned and issued at different dates from 1965 to 1969, and worn indiscriminately alongside the original US-made components, few Diggers being aware of the difference.

British 1937 & 1944 Patterns

Adding further to the confusion of items worn in the average Australian/ New Zealand belt kit were a number of older styles of equipment that found

Australian production M1956 equipment – note contrasting nylon edging: all components are dated between 1968 and 1971. Belt and suspenders are virtually identical to the US originals apart from makers' marks. The 'large' ammunition pouches – note Ordnance arrows – are basically expanded versions of the originals with minor differences; they retain grenade attachments at the sides, and the rear strap connecting to a D-ring on the shoulder harness. A compass/dressing case and toggle rope are attached to the pouches. The 'bum pack' is modelled on the M1961, and incorporates a rubberized collar; clipped to its right side is a 'hutchie' individual shelter in its rubberized carrier in green/brown camouflage finish. Two one-quart plastic canteens are carried high, by slide-keepers; belt hooks on these and the SLR bayonet frog also allowed a lower position. The 'field pack, canvas' or 'large pack' was introduced in 1968; the first version is illustrated – a later type had external webbing strips for additional stowage. The pack is essentially an upper and a lower compartment, with two side pockets, and attachments for the entrenching tool on the flaps. (Private collection)

Webbing and pack carried by Tony Blake of 7RAR in 1970 – a representative individual load made up from items of various origins. The ARVN rucksack, with two external pockets, is mounted on a US lightweight rucksack frame; above it are three Australian M1956 canteens, and the folding sectional satchel in front of them is a US 'case, medical'. Clipped to the right of the pack is an Australian 'large' M1956 pouch with an attached M18 coloured smoke grenade. In the foreground is Blake's belt kit, based on M1956 belt and suspenders. A pair of 44 Pattern pouches flank three more M1956 canteen carriers on wire belt hooks; centrally, note the blackened 37 Pattern bayonet frog – various web items, blackened for parade use (e.g. belt, rifle sling, gaiters) were later reissued for field use. Resting on the webbing at right is an Australian-made collapsible two-quart water bladder in its green/brown camouflage rubberized cover. Top right is a bag for the US M18A1 Claymore anti-personnel mine, with a spool of light-coloured demolition cord beside it.

favour for various reasons. Firstly, on a practical level the inadequate capacity of the US M1956 ammunition pouch led to the hurried reissue of British 37 and 44 Pattern pouches. These were common among soldiers armed with the SLR before the introduction of the Australian 'large' M1956 pouch addressed the problem in 1968. The 37 Pattern 'basic pouches' were of British, Canadian and Australian manufacture, dating from the 1940s through the late 1950s, in their original khaki state or redyed jungle-green. A larger version was the Australian-made 'Pouch, Basic, Large (Aust)', part of the late WWII Australian jungle kit and commonly called 'Bren pouches'. These were identical in design to the basic pouches but significantly wider and deeper; they too came in both khaki and JG versions.

Although the 37 Pattern pouches solved the SLR magazine problem they were not compatible with the M1956 equipment, and a certain amount of personal ingenuity had to be employed to marry the two. Some Diggers cut slits in the rear of the pouch for the belt to pass through; others made use of wire and string – generally a makeshift and unsatisfactory arrangement. More popular were the large 44 Pattern ammunition pouches, which were readily adapted to the M1956 equipment and could be configured to hang low on the belt. These 44 Pattern pouches were British-made – Australia had never undertaken manufacture of the set – and were available to those who had access to the British supply system in Malaysia. The 44 Pattern equipment also had something of an 'old soldier' kudos that appealed to the young Diggers.

Similarly, the 44 Pattern water bottle and carrier were much sought after throughout the war, being especially popular with SASR. The carrier hung well below the level of the belt in a manner that was actually at odds with the current view that items on the belt kit should ride high and tight to the body (the US M1956 set was designed on this principle). A loop and belt hanger allowed the carrier to be hung in two positions, and there was a small internal pocket designed to take a Milbank filter bag. When the M1956 carrier was redesigned for Australian service the low-slinging element of the 44 Pattern cover was reintroduced.

One item of equipment synonymous with the Australian soldier is the 'Fibre Rope Assembly, Single Leg, Polyester Fibre, 1inch Circ, 9 Ft Long' – more simply known as the 'toggle rope'. By the time of Vietnam the actual wooden toggle was no longer attached to one end, and the simple

(continued on page 41)

ROYAL AUSTRALIAN REGIMENT, 1965–66
1: Private, 1RAR, 1965
2: M60 machine-gunner, 5RAR, 1966
3: Staff sergeant, 1RAR, 1965
4: Australian Military Forces patch

A

AUSTRALIAN ARMY TRAINING TEAM VIETNAM
1: WO2 W.Shennan, 1965   2: Capt R.Clarke, 1964   3: WO2 J.D.Roy, 1965
4: Capt P.Jarratt, 1964   5: WO2 A.B.McCloskey, 1st Mobile Strike Force Bn
6 & 7: AATTV shoulder patch & beret badge

B

ANZAC TRAINING TEAMS
1: WO2 B.Lichtwark, 1 NZATTV
2: WO2 R.S.Simpson VC, AATTV
3: Capt I.Teague, AATTV
4: WO2 C.N.McEvoy, AATTV
5: WO2 E.C.Burns, AATTV
6: WO2 S.F.Reid, AATTV

C

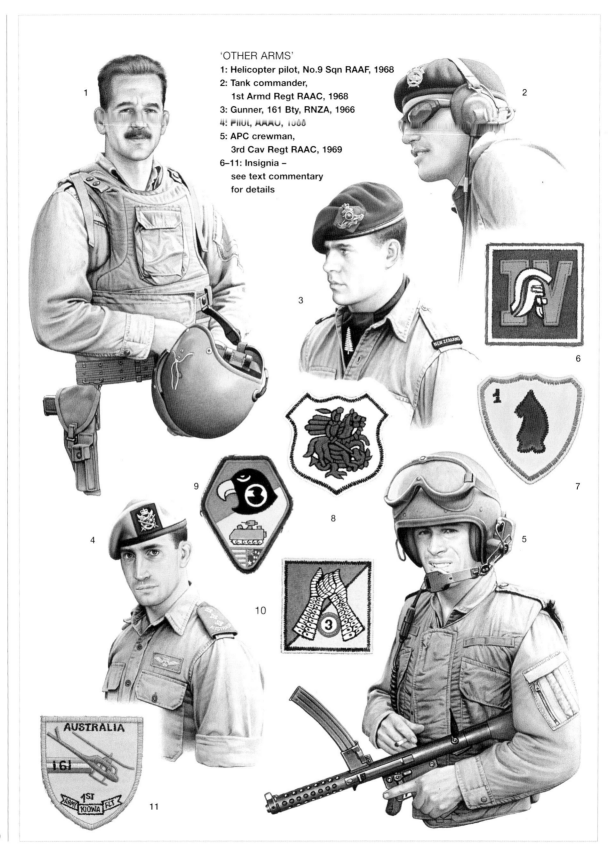

'OTHER ARMS'
1: Helicopter pilot, No.9 Sqn RAAF, 1968
2: Tank commander,
   1st Armd Regt RAAC, 1968
3: Gunner, 161 Bty, RNZA, 1966
4: Pilot, AAAC, 1968
5: APC crewman,
   3rd Cav Regt RAAC, 1969
6–11: Insignia –
   see text commentary
   for details

D

MID-WAR INFANTRY
1: Grenadier, Victor 2 Coy, 1 RNZIR, 1967
2: Private, Whiskey 1 Coy, 1 RNZIR, 1968
3: Signaller, 6RAR, 1970
4: Private, Victor 1 Coy, 1 RNZIR, 1967
5: Unofficial patch, Whiskey 1 Coy

E

SPECIAL AIR SERVICE
1: Patrol member, 3 Sqn SASR, 1969
2: Patrol member, 2 Sqn SASR, 1971
3: Corporal, 2 Sqn SASR, 1971
4: Patrol member, 2 Sqn SASR, 1971

F

SPECIAL AIR SERVICE
1: Patrol member, 4 Tp NZSAS, 1970
2: Patrol member, 1 Sqn SASR, 1968
3: Trooper, 4 Tp NZSAS, 1969
4: Patrol member, 3 Sqn SASR, 1967

G

ROYAL AUSTRALIAN REGIMENT, 1969–72
1: Private, 6RAR, 1969
2: Private, 3RAR, 1971
3: Private, 8RAR, 1970

H

length of green cord was typically coiled into a tight hank and hung from an ammunition pouch.

Machetes of various types were commonly seen in Anzac units, at least one per patrol, although their use was less widespread than in American units due to the stricter doctrine regarding the noise factor. Older WWII British types were the most often seen, together with US styles and the occasional native equivalent from Malaya or Borneo. In 1968 an Australian machete was introduced to complement the M1956 equipment; the sheath was manufactured from the familiar light green canvas, and incorporated a small pocket containing a sharpening stone.

Packs

No rucksack was issued with the US M1956 equipment, and the small 'butt-pack' was clearly insufficient for lengthy patrols. As an emergency measure a hurried reissue was made of 1937 Pattern large packs, essentially the same item as originally issued with the British 1908 Pattern equipment. These packs were largely Australian made of WWII vintage, complete with detachable shoulder-straps and narrower supporting straps. Some packs were hurriedly dyed jungle-green, but as many were issued undyed, and khaki packs were often worn in Vietnam.

It became common practice among Australian troops to carry the folding entrenching tool by wedging the blade beneath the pack flap and securing the helve with the two crossed supporting straps. Additional canteens were often carried on the sides of the pack by the simple expedient of cutting slits in the bag and pushing the cover's slide-keepers through – another example of the Anzac's ability to 'bodgie' his kit in order to overcome shortcomings.

The 44 Pattern haversack was less commonly seen, but was popular among those who could get hold of one. This 44 Pattern pack, though no bigger than the 08/37 model, had the advantage that it had external fittings designed to take items such as the entrenching tool and machete.

Naturally, US packs of all varieties were in great demand from the outset and were the subject of much bartering. The 'Lightweight Rucksack and Frame' was especially popular, and it was not unusual to see a Digger with both 37 Pattern and US lightweight packs fitted simultaneously to the latter's aluminium frame. In June 1966, 5RAR requested a bulk purchase of the lightweight rucksack frame for the carriage of the PRC-25 radio set; Australian 'Sigs', like their American counterparts, had quickly identified the frame as being ideally suited to their particular load.

Although the 08/37 Pattern pack served its purpose initially, there was clearly a requirement for an improved Australian pack. In 1968 the 'Field Pack, Canvas, Olive Drab, 18in x 14in x 7in' was introduced, and generally termed the 'Australian large pack'. Constructed in the usual

Operation 'Atherton', September 1967: Cpl Ivor Briggs, 2RAR, photographed wearing an apparently complete set of US M1967 nylon 'modernised load carrying equipment' (MLCE). Designed specifically to meet needs identified in Vietnam, the M1967 set substituted nylon for the M1956's canvas web, and plastic for its metal fittings. It saw only limited issue, usually in separate components such as pouches and suspenders, and rarely much before 1969. The use of a complete set in 1967 is interesting, and presumably the result of Australian requests for examples to field-trial in Vietnam.

Late and well-worn equipment set used by a New Zealand SAS man, shown from the rear to illustrate personal modifications. The M1956 belt and suspenders are unchanged except that the former is fitted with a Davis quick-release buckle. The four Australian M1956 'large pouches' have all been modified by the removal of the metal slide-keepers and addition of large cloth belt loops. The outer pair are configured to hang low; the one on the right has a small leatherette pouch for a sharpening stone stitched to its side. Two canteens are worn: at right an unmodified M1956, at left a British 44 Pattern fitted with belt loops to ride higher than usual. All components have been camouflage-painted in greens, browns and black. (Private collection)

lightweight green canvas, the design of the pack was unlike anything in current use. It was essentially two large compartments stacked one above the other, with two smaller side pockets. The lower section was meant for the sleeping gear while the upper section was for radios, etc. The padded shoulder straps and integral pads on the pack's front surface gave a degree of comfort. An attachment was provided for the entrenching tool carrier, and a carrying handle and a plastic window for the owner's details, similar to those on the butt-pack, were also included. Although a definite improvement on the WWII vintage packs, the Australian large pack was not well received, and most Diggers would continue to opt for a US pack whenever possible.

Carried either in the pack or in its own rubberized, camouflaged belt pouch was the 'Shelter, Individual' or 'hutchie', the Australian version of the poncho. This, together with a sectional pneumatic mattress and cover, were the Digger's basic sleeping gear. The inflatable mattress sections were of black plastic, three sections fitting into the cloth case to make a single mattress; dividing it into three separate sections meant that it could still be used if one of the sections was punctured. A sleeping bag liner was issued as part of the sleeping gear but rarely used; the useful and lightweight 'Net, Mosquito, Field' was more commonly carried. The Australians had many years' experience in dealing with the perils of mosquito-borne diseases, and most Diggers had a 'mozzie-net' somewhere in their gear.

Rations

Field rations in Vietnam were either US C-Rations or the Australian '24 Hour (One Man) Ration Pack'. The latter was more akin to British 'Compo' rations, and contained such familiar delights as 'cereal block' and 'corned beef'. Each 24-hour pack consisted of breakfast, lunch and tea (supper) sections, as well as a sundries pack containing chocolate, glucose tablets, condensed milk, sugar, tea, salt, margarine, water-sterilizing tablets, matches and toilet paper. Unique to the Australian ration pack was the combination spoon/can opener, as was the British-designed 'Hexamine' solid fuel stove with its wax paper-covered blocks. The issue of US or Australian field rations was dependent on the prevailing supply situation, and doubtless both varieties were cursed in equal proportions by the Diggers who were on the receiving end.

Munitions

Ammunition for both 7.62mm SLR and 5.56mm M16 rifles was loaded into magazines and placed in pouches on the belt kit. It was not Anzac

practice to carry loose ammunition, and while cloth magazine bandoliers in both calibres were manufactured and issued they were far less commonly seen than in American units. Australia also manufactured the individual cloth bandoliers for the 100-round machine gun ammunition belts, but again, these were rarely seen. Belts were more typically carried loose around the body protected in plastic sleeves, or folded into the basic pouches. The practice of cutting up air mattress sections to make sleeves for ammunition belts became commonplace, so much so that a purpose-made plastic sleeve was eventually introduced. While the sleeves did protect the ammunition from dirt they also caused condensation and corrosion, and could be awkward if the belt was required in an emergency; although the practice had both advocates and detractors, it became a distinct Anzac trademark in Vietnam.

US-made M72 LAWs (light anti-tank weapons), M18A1 Claymore mines, and the whole range of signalling and fragmentation grenades were issued to Anzac troops, and were carried on the equipment in the same manner as in American service.

NEW ZEALAND UNIFORMS & EQUIPMENT

It was decided for logistical reasons that the New Zealand contingent at Nui Dat should be linked into the 1ATF supply system. Standardizing equipment with the Australians obviously simplified the logistics within the Task Force; however, the Kiwis were keen to maintain a sense of national identity, and some differences were to be seen.

Victor 1 Company deployed to Vietnam straight from Terendak Camp in Malaysia, where they had been supplied by the 28th Commonwealth Brigade. They arrived wearing British flannel shirts and British 'JGs', which were considered the best type available; when these wore out they were replaced by Australian 'greens' from 1ATF stocks. Later in the war a distinct New Zealand-made JG uniform was produced and worn alongside the Australian version. The New Zealand JG shirt buttoned full-length, but retained the British-style pleated pocket with V-shaped flap. The NZ Defence Department adopted the Australian tropical combat uniform in 1967, and these were also made under contract in New Zealand, the uniforms being identical to those made in Australia.

A New Zealand pattern combat boot was occasionally seen alongside the Australian GP boots, of similar construction but featuring 'speed-lace' hooks instead of the upper rows of lace holes. These were rare, however; most Kiwis wore GP boots, or American J-boots if they could get them. New Zealand even produced its own version of the standard JG jungle hat from 1968, though Australian and British hats were also issued. The New Zealand version was recognizable by small snap fasteners on both sides which allowed the brim to be worn up in 'cowboy' fashion. A practice that seems to have been peculiar to the Kiwi contingent was adding a chin strap from a length of bootlace or para-cord.

New Zealand personal equipment in Vietnam largely reflected the trends of the prevailing Australian issue. There were, however, certain

June 1968: Pte Graham Ilsley of 4RAR at the village of Binh Ba. Issue of tropical JGs was well established by this date, although the mixing of both patterns would continue throughout the war. In practice the field dressing pockets on the sleeves were found to be just the right size for a packet of cigarettes. His hat is Australian-made; and by mid-1968 both US- and Australian-made components of M1956 webbing were in use. Here a 'universal' ammunition pouch and a toggle rope are attached to the 'bum pack'; two canteens are worn on the hip, and a pair of British 44 Pattern 'basic' pouches at the front. Note that the SLR has both the new plastic carrying handle but the old triangular-section handguard.

43

distinctions: for instance, there was a greater use of British 44 Pattern webbing in the New Zealand companies due to the Kiwis' closer working relations with the British Army at that time. The original Victor 1 Coy had received 44 Pattern equipment at Terendak, and though re-equipped with the US M1956 set the New Zealanders continued to favour the British design. In particular, the large basic pouches, water bottles and haversack were common in New Zealand service. By contrast the use of the older 37 Pattern basic pouches was not a feature of Kiwi webbing. The New Zealanders received the Australian-modified M1956 items as they came into service, and generally mirrored the evolution of Australian personal equipment, though perhaps at a slightly slower rate.

Although the Kiwis shared the Australians' reluctance to adorn their field JGs with any form of insignia, Victor 1 did have a black cravat/scarf made up by an Asian tailor shop. An original member of Victor 1 recalls that these were given out in two versions, silk for No.1 Dress and cotton for everyday wear, both being embroidered with a small white Kiwi motif (see Plate E1). These were worn in the open neck of 'best' JGs, or loose around the neck in the field; photographs show some members of Victor 2 wearing the scarf bandanna-style around the jungle hat. (161 Battery RNZA also had black scarves made up in theatre, theirs featuring a white fern-leaf motif – see Plate D3.) Berets were worn with 'best' JGs: green in 1RNZIR, dark blue in RNZA, and airborne maroon in NZSAS, with the relevant cap badge centred over the left eye.

A unique order of dress in the New Zealand Army is the 'Dacron' uniform worn as a summer barracks/walking-out uniform, similar to the

NZ infantrymen in typical 1970 period equipment (and hairstyles – note the sideburns). The foreground soldier, perhaps a platoon commander (note the compass and the map in its 'talc' cover, attached to 'idiot cords' round his neck), wears standard Australian JGs and a New Zealand hat. His webbing is M1956 with British 44 Pattern pouches; his second-type 'large pack' has eyeletted strips of webbing for attaching additional items. The signaller beyond him wears a New Zealand JG shirt identifiable by pleated pockets, with the sleeves roughly shortened; his NZ hat shows the identifying press studs allowing the brim to be snapped upright. It was standard practice in Anzac units for platoon commanders and signallers to carry the M16. (NZ Army PR)

Australian tan summer dress. 'Dacrons' were a lightweight shirt and trousers in a distinctive chocolate brown shade. The shirt was typically short-sleeved, worn open-necked and outside the trousers; normal rank insignia were worn on the sleeves and shoulder straps, and the New Zealand Forces Overseas patch was commonly displayed on the right shoulder. Dacrons were rarely worn in Vietnam, being restricted (like the Australian 'tan' uniform) to transit flights in and out of theatre.

Australian & New Zealand insignia

Both Australia and New Zealand followed British Army rank practice for commissioned and non-commissioned ranks. Officers wore their **rank** on detachable 'slides', simple JG sleeves that slipped over the shoulder straps of the shirt. Earlier slides typically featured full-sized 'pips' and crowns in either embroidered or metal form, often with a coloured backing depending on the wearer's arm of service – scarlet for infantry, yellow for armour, etc. Later slides were manufactured with directly embroidered pips and crowns in smaller 'subdued' form for field use. Some slides additionally included curved **titles** at their base, either embroidered or metal. Those of individual units – 'RAAC', 'AAAC', etc. – were occasionally seen, but officially only a generic national title was sanctioned to be worn while serving overseas.

Non-commissioned officers and warrant officers wore flat-embroidered rank insignia on the sleeves following the British sequence. These badges of rank, especially those of warrant officers, were often applied to a JG 'brassard' which slipped over one arm and was secured under the end of the shoulder strap. Military Police from the Provost companies wore the traditional 'MP' brassard. The Australian's attitude to the spit-and-polish appearance of 'base bludgers' is illustrated by the reaction to a young Military Police corporal's appearance at Fire Support Base Coral in May 1968. There to take charge of some of the enemy prisoners from the night's heavy fighting, he is described thus: 'In his freshly starched greens, spitty boots and brassard made in Shop Three in Baria or wherever, he looked a right spiv.'

The 'Australian Military Forces' **overseas patch**, known as the 'Rising Sun', was authorized to be worn by all members of the Task Force, but its use was sporadic even within a single unit. The patch was a continuation of a design that dated back to the Boer War of 1901, and was worn as a general service badge by Australians in both World Wars as bronze hat and collar devices. The scroll had read 'Australian Commonwealth Military Forces' until 1949, when it was changed to its Vietnam-era wording. The 1966 AMF Dress Manual described the patch as 'Two inches square and woven on washable material – the upper edge is to be placed horizontally half an inch below the centre of the shoulder seam or the lower edge of the United States Distinguished Unit Citation if worn'. (This US award had been presented to 3RAR for service in the Korean War and was worn by all ranks of the battalion.)

September 1967: Cpl Heinz Grabowski of 2RAR – who had previously served in the French Foreign Legion – patrols against a typical background of Phuoc Tuy rubber trees. There seem to have been no hard and fast rules about the wear of rank insignia and the AMF 'Rising Sun' patch on field JGs, and both were occasionally seen, as here. As a section commander he carries a lensatic compass in its M1956 case on one shoulder suspender, additionally secured with a lanyard.

Lanyards in corps, regimental and battalion colours were worn with the tan Summer Dress and occasionally seen on 'best' JGs during transit and parades; the lanyard was a simple length of cord worn around the left shoulder and terminating in the shirt pocket. A few of the more commonly seen examples were: RAAC, yellow; RAA, white; and SASR, Garter blue. The individual battalions of the Royal Australian Regiment wore lanyards in the following colours:

1RAR, Garter blue; 2RAR, black; 3RAR, Rifle green; 4RAR, scarlet; 5RAR, gold; 6RAR, khaki; 7RAR, maroon; 8RAR, slate grey.

The First Battalion, Royal **New Zealand** Infantry Regiment traditionally wore a small red diamond patch on the upper left sleeve in some orders of dress, and this was very occasionally seen on JGs in Vietnam. A locally-made patch of a red diamond featuring a white Kiwi over a *taiaha* (Maori spear) was worn on a very limited basis by members of Whiskey 1 Company (see Plate E).

SAS FIELD DRESS

In traditional SAS fashion, the Australian and New Zealand squadrons in Vietnam were given a free hand in their choice of operational equipment. Individual modification of field gear was encouraged, with each trooper putting together a set of equipment that met his personal combat needs. It is, however, a fallacy that SAS units had instant and unlimited access to the latest and most exotic equipment and weaponry. In Vietnam the squadrons had to indent for items through normal channels, and acquired a high proportion of their stores through the traditional methods of 'begging, borrowing and stealing'.

Because of close working relationships with various allied special forces units, some items could be acquired through those channels; others were sourced from Asian countries where the SAS trained and operated, such as Thailand and Singapore. Many SASR men had worked alongside their British counterparts of 22 SAS Regiment, and consequently there was a significant amount of 44 Pattern webbing in the squadrons, the large water bottles in particular being an SAS favourite.

The post of SASR LO (Liaison Officer) was specially created to provide the squadrons with a point of contact with foreign units and agencies such as the CIA. One of the LO's main functions was the procurement of equipment and spare parts which were outside of the normal supply system – 'off the books', in SASR parlance. Another way of obtaining special purpose items was to request a squadron trial with a view to future procurement. At the conclusion of the trial the squadron would submit their report and somehow neglect to return the items in question, the rule of thumb being that once something went into squadron stores it stayed there.

Though a small number of indigenous 'tiger-stripe' uniforms were worn, the US ERDL Camouflage Tropical Combat Uniform quickly emerged as standard SASR operational dress in Vietnam, and would remain so throughout the regiment's involvement (and long after). The Australians called the uniform the 'Seal suit', possibly because of its use by US Navy SEALs with whom SASR sometimes worked. (Confusingly, a few SAS men also acquired the unique inflatable jackets which were synonymous with these elite US Navy commandos and were also called the 'Seal jacket/vest'.) Whatever the origins of the term, a signal dated 26 June 1968 from AHQ to AFV approved the purchase of 200 'Seal suits' for the resident SAS squadron (a footnote to the file explains that the term is a local one). A further signal of 27 December 1969 to 1ATF notes that 'Camouflage suits are now in very short supply and a direct purchase from the US is requested'.

The ERDL uniform was worn by the majority of Australian and New Zealand SAS men; its pattern was considered ideal for most environments, and its multiple pockets suited the amount of kit carried on SAS operations. The light weight of the fabric allowed the suit to dry out overnight at body temperature, although it was reckoned to be good for a maximum of three patrols before becoming unserviceable.

From the outset SASR used a significant number of American equipment items which were considered to be of higher quality than their Australian equivalents. The US Tropical Combat Boots – called 'J-boots' by the Australians – were universally adopted by SAS squadrons. One veteran ruefully admits that 'At one point the only bit of Australian gear that I was using were my ID discs and my hutchie, which says heaps for the quality of Australian-produced gear'. He does, however, concede that Australian-manufactured ammunition was generally superior and used a cleaner-burning powder.

On operations it was standard SAS practice to camouflage every item of equipment as well as the face and hands. Webbing and packs were sprayed and daubed with paint in a variety of patterns in an effort to disrupt the recognisable shapes. The use of face paint was taken very seriously in SASR, and it was always thoroughly applied to any exposed flesh. The American stick-type was the most commonly used, along with some later Australian-made 'compacts'; a base of pale green with darker green or black stripes was typical.

As with individual equipment, the selection of SAS weapons was subject to personal preference, and troopers could ask the squadron armourer for a number of modifications. The standard SLR was adapted in SAS use with the following modifications:
1. Conversion to fully automatic function.
2. 30-round magazine as standard.
3. Removal of flash suppressor, bayonet lugs, sling swivels and carrying handle.
4. Magazine release catch extended.

May 1970: Sgt John Gebhardt of 1 Sqn SASR uses an American AN/URC-64 emergency receiver/transmitter, as used by both downed aircrew and special forces. The jungle hat in ERDL camouflage, with foliage loops and large mesh ventilators, is typical of the variety of headgear bought from local suppliers by both individuals and squadrons. Gebhardt's belt is made from an aircraft cargo tie-down strap with a quick-release roller buckle; these were originally made in Malaya, and their use continued in Vietnam. The large pouch is an example of initiative overcoming shortfalls in issue equipment, in this case the lack of suitable pouches for the 30-rd SLR magazine. It is a five-pocket F1 SMG pouch opened out to make two pockets and flaps.

Additionally, individuals could request a forward pistol grip, and even a pace-counter set into the handguard or stock. Some SLRs in the squadron's inventory were converted to a 'carbine' format by halving the length of the barrel and handguard. Another 'off the books' conversion saw the flash suppressor from an M3 sub-machine gun added, which by all accounts made the rifle sound like a .50cal Browning when fired.

The aim of removing the flash suppressor and 'chopping' the barrel was to deliberately maximize the weapon's muzzle flash and signature when fired. The small SAS patrol had to be capable of fighting its way clear of any contact with a larger enemy force, switching instantly from a stealthy covert posture to one of noisy aggression. Consequently SAS patrols were extremely heavily armed and carried prodigious amounts of ammunition. When a patrol was compromised, contact drills called for sudden and overwhelming firepower to cover its withdrawal; in such situations accuracy of fire was secondary to volume – the aim was to stun and confuse the enemy in the first seconds of a contact, by creating as much noise and muzzle flash as possible. If the five-man patrol could momentarily give the impression of being a much larger force they could extricate themselves before the enemy realised their mistake.

GLOSSARY OF ANZAC TERMS

This is a short selection of official acronyms, with a very few of the unofficial terms used in Vietnam.

AAAC Australian Army Aviation Corps

AATTV Australian Army Training Team Vietnam

AFV Australian Force Vietnam

AHQ Army Headquarters

ALSG Australian Logistic Support Group

ATF (1ATF) (1st) Australian Task Force

AMF Australian Military Forces

ANZAC Australian and New Zealand Army Corps

ANZUS Australia, New Zealand and US Treaty (1951)

Balmy Ba Vietnamese beer – a corruption of the leading brand name.

Base bludgers Rear echelon personnel – derogatory term used by front line troops (Anzac equivalent of US 'REMF').

Bushman Scouts 'Turned' Viet Cong who surrendered under the Chieu Hoi ('Open Arms') programme and served as scouts for 1ATF (equivalent to US 'Kit Carson Scouts')

Digger Traditional name for the Australian soldier – its origin is disputed.

FSPB Fire Support Patrol Base – an Anzac refinement of the US Fire Base, implying a more pro-active approach. It served the dual purpose of providing both a semi-permanent home for artillery units and a base from which aggressive infantry patrolling was pursued.

Harbour A temporary defensive position.

Hutchie Plasticized tent sheet, Australian equivalent of the US 'poncho' – and by extension, the infantryman's sleeping shelter (also 'basha').

HQAAFV Headquarters Australian Army Force Vietnam, based in Saigon

Horseshoe The initial New Zealand Company position in 1967, located some 8km east of the main base at Nui Dat, from which patrols and sweeps were mounted in the surrounding countryside.

Another photo of Sgt Gebhardt. His brown/green camouflage net scarf is the older British type commonly seen in SASR use. His US lightweight rucksack frame has been cut down and the nylon bag repositioned high on the back. A further pair of lightweight rucksack straps have been adapted as a shoulder harness; the taped-on waterproof pouch probably carries the AN/URC radio. The 'chopped' SLR illustrates several SAS practices – the removal of sling swivels and carrying handle, and a (particularly neat) camouflage paint pattern. Although there is no external evidence, the rifle has almost certainly been converted for full automatic fire, with a pin inserted to hold the working parts to the rear on an empty magazine.

HQV Headquarters Vietnam Force (NZ)

Kiwi Traditional name for a New Zealander, after the flightless bird which is employed as a national motif

Luscombe Field The 1ATF airstrip at Nui Dat

Nasho National Serviceman, i.e. a conscript/draftee rather than a career regular soldier

NEWZAD New Zealand Army Detachment Vietnam

NZSAS New Zealand Special Air Service

OMC Owen Machine Carbine (Aust sub-machine gun)

OR Other ranks (US, 'enlisted personnel')

Q-stores Quartermaster stores

RAA Royal Australian Artillery

RAAC Royal Australian Armoured Corps

RAAF Royal Australian Air Force

RAN Royal Australian Navy

R & R Rest and Recreation – out-of-theatre leave; each soldier was allocated one week-long R and R during his year's tour of duty.

R in C Rest in Country – in-theatre leave

RNZA Royal New Zealand Artillery

RNZIR Royal New Zealand Infantry Regiment

RNZAMC Royal New Zealand Army Medical Corps

RTA Return to Australia

RTNZ Return to New Zealand

Sapper Military engineer (British/Anzac)

SEATO South East Asia Treaty Organization

Section Smallest tactical unit in British/Anzac armies – approx 10 men (US 'squad')

SASR Special Air Service Regiment (Aust)

SLR Self Loading Rifle – the L1A1 7.62mm gas operated, magazine fed, semi-automatic rifle, the standard Anzac infantry weapon throughout the war.

Trooper Stephen Rodgers of 1 Sqn patrols in dense jungle. The ERDL camouflage uniform is worn with a Vietnamese-made beret in matching fabric – a popular choice in SASR. Its multi-stitched shoulder straps identify his pack as a captured NVA rucksack or a local copy. His belt kit is typically eccentric: a belt made from some kind of 37 Pattern strap, with single pockets cut from a US BAR belt and adapted to hang low on the hips.

May 1970: a patrol from 1 Sqn return to Nui Dat courtesy of a UH-1B of No.9 Sqn RAAF. Patrol commander Sgt John O'Keefe (foreground) has a cargo-strap belt with both large and small SAS pouches, and a compass case. He wears the Australian 'large pack' – not very popular in SASR, but used late in the war. The expanding cargo pockets and loose cut of the US camouflage uniform made it ideal for long SAS patrols when carrying capacity was at a premium, and items such as water bladders could be stowed inside the coat. The trooper at left, holding a long 30-rd SLR magazine, has the same belt kit as O'Keefe but a Bergan rucksack. The uncropped photo shows the other three members of the patrol armed with an M79, an XM148, and an M16 for the signaller.

Fine study of a New Zealand SAS patrol member, c1969/70; the noticeably clean ERDL uniform suggests that the photo was taken at the start of the mission. His web gear is M1956 with at least one low-slung SAS pouch; hung from his harness are M67 'baseball', M18 smoke and M34 white phosphorus grenades. Note the special SAS patrol gloves – see Plate F1. His SLR has typical modifications: most obviously, the removal of the carrying handle, sling swivels and flash suppressor. (NZ Army PR)

Stand-to The period at first and last light when a unit is on high alert in case of enemy attack – an old British Army practice.

TAOR Tactical Area of Responsibility

Uc Dai Loi Vietnamese for 'Australian'

Ulu The bush, from the Malay term (US 'the boonies')

Up the guts Australian term for direct frontal assault

V Force Vietnam Force (NZ)

Wallaby Airlines 35 Transport Sqn RAAF, which flew from Vung Tau

Wheel Australian slang for an officer

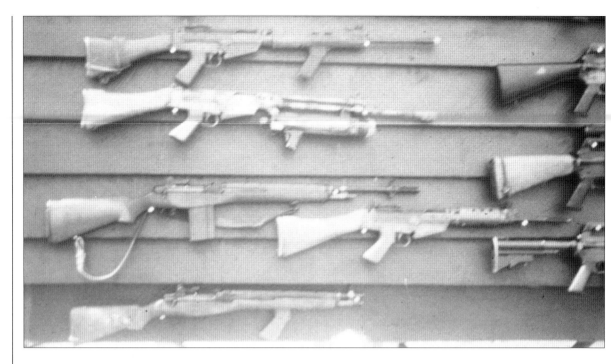

Although out of focus, this photograph still shows an interesting display of weapons by 2 Sqn SASR at SAS Hill, Nui Dat in 1970.

(Top) An SLR with carrying handle, flash suppressor and sling swivels removed, and a forward pistol grip added.

(Second) All the usual modifications, plus entire forearm removed, and XM148 40mm grenade launcher added.

(Third) US M14, apparently unmodified – it used the same 7.62mm ammunition as the SLR, but its presence in the SASR inventory at this date is unexplained.

(Fourth) SLR with barrel, gas return and forearm 'chopped' by the squadron armourer, reducing overall length by about 12ins – often referred to as the 'carbine' version. Rails for mounting a telescopic sight have been welded to the top cover.

(Bottom) Another M14, this one subjected to a barrel-chop, and with an SLR pistol grip added to the handguard.

SELECT BIBLIOGRAPHY

ANON:

Australian Military Forces Dress Manual, Army HQ, Canberra (1963)

The First Battalion Royal New Zealand Infantry Regiment Journal, HQ 1RNZIR, Singapore (1983)

The Special Air Service Regiment, Australian Army Publications, Victoria (1967)

Battle, M.R., *The Year of the Tiger* (5RAR Yearbook), Printcraft Press, Sydney (1970)

Breen, R., *First to Fight*, Allen & Unwin, Sydney (1988)

Clarke, C.J., *Yours Faithfully* (3RAR Yearbook), Printcraft Press, Sydney (1972)

Clunies-Ross, A., *The Grey Eight in Vietnam* (8RAR Yearbook), Brisbane (1971)

Guest, R., *The Team in Pictures*, AATTV Association, Canberra (1992)

Landers, R., *'Saddle Up'*, New South Wales (1998)

McAulay, L., *The Battle of Long Tan*, Arrow Books

McAulay, L., *The Battle of Coral*, Arrow Books (1988)

McNeil, I., *The Team: Australian Army Advisers in Vietnam 1962–72*, Australian War Memorial, Canberra (1984)

Newman, S.D., *Vietnam Gunners*, Moana Press, NZ (1988)

Roberts, R.R., *The Anzac Battalion 1970–71* (2RAR Yearbook), Printcraft Press, Sydney (1972)

Sisson, C., *Wounded Warriors*, Total Press Ltd, Auckland, NZ (1993)

Smith, C., *The Killing Zone: NZ Infantry in Vietnam 1967–71*, AQU, Auckland, NZ

Subritsky, M., *The Vietnam Scrapbook*, Three Feathers Publishing Co, NZ (1995)

THE PLATES

A: ROYAL AUSTRALIAN REGIMENT, 1965–66

A1: Private, 1RAR, 1965

Old style standard 'jungle greens' are worn, with a British-made jungle hat (identifiable by the large screened ventilation holes), and the Australian net 'sweatrag' with its distinctive oval pattern. 1RAR deployed wearing old leather ankle-length 'Boots AB' or 'Boots AB/TS'; both would be replaced within the year. Much was made at the time of the inadequacy of the ankle boot/gaiter arrangement, which led to the accelerated design and issue of the much improved GP boot. The gaiters were secured with three straps, two on the sides and one under the sole of the boot, and were dyed or polished black to match the boots. Webbing is US-made M1956 supplemented with a pair of green-dyed 37 Pattern basic pouches' on the front of the belt. These older pouches were worn in a number of makeshift ways; they usually hung low on the hips but were also worn – as here – in the correct manner, high on the belt and buckled to the pack straps, thus eliminating the need for a separate shoulder harness. The pack here is an undyed khaki 1908/37 Pattern large pack, probably manufactured in the 1940s or 1950s, with later-style wide shoulder straps. Both khaki and green-dyed packs were used indiscriminately at this early date, although the latter would eventually become general. Note the 'fibre rope assembly' or toggle rope hung from the belt – useful for any number of purposes such as water crossings, prisoner security, and flipping enemy bodies from a safe distance as a precaution against booby-traps. The SLR is an early production weapon fitted with the triangular-section handguard and wooden carrying handle; the field dressing taped to the stock would become a universal Anzac practice, ensuring that a dressing was always quickly to hand.

A2: Machine-gunner, 5RAR, 1966

The jungle hat is still British, the Australian version not being introduced until 1968. Webbing consists of M1956 belt, suspenders and metal canteens, to which are added a pair of 'Pouches Basic, Large' from the WWII Australian jungle kit.

These Australian 'Bren' pouches were popular with machine gun teams for carrying belts of linked ammunition; they featured the same snap closure as the smaller version, and were mainly to be found in khaki, although green examples also existed. A further 100-round belt is draped around the torso protected by a sleeve cut from a section of air mattress, here a green US example. The M60 itself has a short belt loaded; it is fitted with a US web rifle sling, and has the ubiquitous field dressing taped to one of the bipod legs.

A3: Staff sergeant, 1RAR, 1965

This veteran NCO represents the nucleus of experience found within the regular battalion at this date; he is quite likely a veteran of the Korean War and/or the Malayan Emergency, and certainly has many years' South-East Asian service under his belt. The wearing of coloured quick-recognition bands around the jungle hat had begun with the British in Malaya to identify particular sub-units; in Vietnam the Australians adopted the practice more as a simple 'friend or foe' device. Webbing is typical for this period, a mix of US-made M1956 and older British components; the use of both 08/37 Pattern pack and M1956 'bum-pack' together was common until a superior US pack could be acquired. The 1908/37 Pattern large pack is a standard khaki example that has been dyed green as a so-called 'emergency issue'. These packs of 1940s/50s Australian or Canadian manufacture were essentially copies of the British WWI pack, complete with narrow supporting straps which were also dyed green. The slide-keepers of an M1956 canteen have been inserted through slits cut in the sides of the pack. Canteens at this stage were both the old M1910 metal type and the M1956 plastic, either US-made or the greener Australian copies. The M1961 Combination Entrenching Tool was often carried as depicted. The 9mm Owen 'machine carbine' was in the process of being replaced by the F1 9mm SMG and the M16 rifle, although it was highly regarded by experienced soldiers and would be retained well into 1966. Some WWII vintage Owens were painted in a green/yellow camouflage pattern, but by 1965 the majority had been up-graded and a plain black finish was more common. The Owen's 33-round round box magazines are carried in old

The two patterns of JG shirt. (Right) the first or 'standard greens' type, worn throughout the period; this example, dated 1967, has the 'Rising Sun' overseas patch, and brass 'Australia' titles on JG shoulder strap slides. (Left) the 'tropical JG' shirt, with two sleeve pockets and slanted breast pockets; meant to be worn outside the trousers, it was cut shorter and squarer at the hem than the original pattern. This is in fact an NZ-manufactured example, identified by the large white spec-tag inside the collar; it bears white-on-black 'New Zealand' title slides. (Private collection)

Three types of jungle hat worn in Vietnam.
(Top left) British, with large mesh ventilators.
(Centre) Australian, made from 1968; more steeply sloped brim, and simple eyelet ventilators.
(Right) New Zealand, this example dated 1970; the NZ hat tended to be cut more fully, and had press-studs to fasten up both sides of the brim. (Private collection)

khaki 37 Pattern basic pouches modified to hang low on the belt; a purpose-made five-pocket magazine pouch was made for the Owen, but rarely seen.

A4: Australian Military Forces patch

The AMF patch was known as the 'Rising Sun' due both to its design – a fan-shape of blades – and to its similarity to the label of a well-known brand of Australian jam (for a fuller account of the device's origins, see MAA 123, *The Australian Army at War*). Officially to be worn on the left shoulder of the JG shirt by all ranks, its issue was less than universal and its display was never rigorously enforced.

B: AUSTRALIAN ARMY TRAINING TEAM VIETNAM

B1: WO2 Wayne Shennan, 1965

Shennan served as an adviser to an ARVN Ranger battalion in I Corps, and is depicted in their uniform. The ERDL poplin camouflage shirt is cut in a style unique to the ARVN Rangers, with shoulder straps and reinforced shoulders. Below the Team patch are Australian parachute wings and the crown rank badge of warrant officer second class. Above the right pocket is a pin-on ARVN Ranger qualification badge in cast brass with silvered swords and star. The Ranger beret is garnet (maroon) and worn pulled left in the Vietnamese/French fashion, with the bullion-embroidered winged sword badge over the right eye.

B2: Captain Rex Clarke, Advisory Team Seven; Phu Bai National Training Centre, 1964

Clarke was known to have an interest in heraldry and insignia, and wears an eclectic combination of badges on his privately acquired US Tropical Combat Uniform. AATTV was initially fitted into the existing framework of advisers under the command of the US Military Assistance Command Vietnam (MACV), and that organization's left shoulder patch was adopted by a few early Team members like Clarke. The shoulder slides bearing embroidered captain's rank and brass national titles are Australian, as are the parachute wings, here the heavy embroidered type for service dress worn in the British/ Australian manner on the right arm. Silk-embroidered Vietnamese parachute wings are worn above

the left breast pocket (contrary to US practice, which placed all foreign qualification awards on the right breast), and a Vietnamese Training Centre patch is worn in a clear plastic 'pocket hanger'. Like many Team members, Clarke has retained his slouch hat as the single most identifiable feature of Australian uniform.

B3: WO2 J.D.Roy, Darlac Province, 1965

Roy was a member of Capt Barry Petersen's team working with Rhade and M'Nong *Montagnards* in the Central Highlands. The 'Beo Gam' or 'leopard' pattern uniform found favour with many American and Australian Special Forces during the early years, though its use would become less common as the more popular 'tiger-stripe' and subsequent American camouflage uniforms became available. On his green beret is the pressed metal badge specially made for the Troung Son Force ('Great Mountain' Force).

B4: Captain Peter Jarratt, 1964

The Vietnamese tailorshop 'tiger-stripe' uniform was available in a wide variety of styles and, like the 'leopard' pattern, was popular with those Team members who accompanied their indigenous units on field operations. All advisers quickly adopted the dress of their particular host unit, both as a sign of solidarity and to avoid being singled out by enemy marksmen. The long-peaked field cap in 'leopard' camouflage, styled after the US field cap of the 1950s, was most typical of this early period. Webbing is of US origin and includes an M1943 Browning Automatic Rifle belt supported by M1956 suspenders; SF troops appreciated the carrying capacity of the BAR belt's six large pockets. The M16 rifle is an early production model with modified bolt-assist but still with the first type three-pronged flash supressor.

B5: WO2 A.B.McCloskey, 212 Company, 1st Mobile Strike Force Battalion

The company- and battalion-sized 'Mike Force' units were made up of *Montagnards* commanded by USSF teams, and were principally tasked with relieving SF outposts throughout I Corps. McCloskey's uniform thus reflects USSF influence; Australians who worked with USSF in the Mike Forces were accorded the privilege of wearing the famous green beret, a hitherto unprecedented gesture of professional esteem on the part of the Americans. On the US-made rifle-green beret is worn the 'flash' of the 5th Special Forces Group (Airborne), to which all USSF personnel in Vietnam were assigned; the Australians would add the badge of their parent unit, here the 'Skippy' of the Royal Australian Regiment. A final pattern US Tropical Combat Coat, with the AATTV patch, is worn over an American OD undershirt.

B6: AATTV shoulder patch
B7: AATTV beret badge
In July 1966, LtCol A.Miller, then CO of AATTV, asked WO2 Laurie Nicholson to design a team badge; Nicholson had no particular expertise in this area, but was temporarily attached to HQ in Saigon following a spell in hospital. His design was based on the insignia of MACV to which AATTV had strong ties. The colours chosen were green to symbolize the tropical environment, and yellow/red to reflect the flag of the Republic of Vietnam – as well as being the colours most commonly associated with Australia. The two native weapons, the Australian boomerang and the *Montagnard* crossbow, referred to the Team's work with indigenous peoples; and 'Persevere' was chosen as the official Team motto. In 1967 the Commander Australian Forces Vietnam authorized the wearing of the patch on the right shoulder of field uniform, although as a 'theatre-specific' item it could not be worn outside Vietnam. The initial batch were made by Kasamaki & Co Ltd in Tokyo, and this contract would be renewed several times during the Team's existence. Vietnamese tailorshop copies were inevitably produced, in both full colour and more rarely in 'subdued' form; but the Japanese version remained the most common and is regarded as the true patch. In October 1969 the badge was officially confirmed as 'Catalogue No. 8455/ NIC/ insignia, shoulder sleeve, AATTV, green'. An AFV file of July 1969 puts the scale of issue at 'five per man, four for wear on uniform and one on a removable brassard'. Another file of September 1969 notes that the patch has been approved as an item of dress and could henceforth be issued at public expense, having previously been procured out of unit funds. In 1970 a metal version of the badge became available, and was worn on a rifle-green beret – this unique headgear was introduced in a bid to standardize Team uniform somewhat and to replace the many and varied indigenous items in use. The locally produced badge was of the Vietnamese 'beer-can' type, so called from the poor quality pressed brass used (the badge would often break at the junction of boomerang and crossbow); it was allowed to dull to a dark patina.

C: ANZAC TRAINING TEAMS
C1: WO2 Brian Lichtwark, 1 NZATTV, 1971
Though some New Zealand warrant officers served with AATTV, the separate 1 NZ Army Training Team Vietnam was formed in January 1971. Its primary task was instructing Regional Forces at the Chi Lang National Training Centre in IV Corps, Vietnam's Southern Delta region. A second NZ team was established in February 1972 at the USSF-run Dong Ba Thin school for Cambodian troops near Cam Rhan Bay. Lichtwark wears NZ-pattern 'greens', which differed only in pocket details from the Australian pattern, with the white-on-black national titles. New Zealand warrant officers were given honorary Vietnamese lieutenant's rank and wore the two 'plum blossoms' on the left collar point, either in pressed brass or embroidered as here. Some additionally had their NZ rank insignia embroidered onto the right chest above a nametape – note the wreathed crown shown here. 1NZATTV approved an 'NZ ARMY' tape to be worn in US fashion above the left pocket. The Chi Lang Training Centre patch, worn on the left sleeve, depicts a flaming arrow set against the sacred Seven Mountains range in the Delta region. Examples studied have been silk-screen printed, but it is likely that silk-embroidered versions were also made.

C2: WO2 R.S.Simpson VC
Ray Simpson's career with AATTV began in 1962 as a member of the original team at the Dong Da Training Centre, and continued with the USSF at Khe Sanh. On a second tour in 1964 he won a Distinguished Conduct Medal while working with USSF. In May 1969 he showed extraordinary courage on two separate occasions while serving with Mike Force units, single-handedly saving and fighting to guard

(Left) Black leather 'Boots, General Purpose', as issued to the vast majority of Anzacs. Based on a Canadian pattern, the GP boots were first tested in 1962 by 2RAR, and issued to AATTV on a limited basis in 1965. Within a year they were general issue to all Australians in theatre; those made by Dunlop, the original contractors, remained the troops' favourite. (Right) Australian-designed short jungle boots – 'Boots, Combat, Wet Weather/Area' – were tested by 1RAR in Vietnam early in 1966; this pair are dated 1968. Though superior to the longer British type they were judged unfit for prolonged field use, and were relegated to wear in base areas. (Private collection)

Australian production 7.62mm L1A1 Self Loading Rifle. First manufactured at Lithgow in 1959, this was essentially indistinguishable from the British model until the green plastic carrying handle was introduced from 1968. This 1969 example has a matt parkerized finish and second-type oval section handguard (the triangular section first type is shown below). Note 20- and 30-rd magazines; bayonet frogs (37 Pattern above M1956 with wire hanger); and cleaning roll with contents – oiler, pullthrough, brush, and combination gas regulator key/ extractor stud/ foresight tool. (Private collection)

wounded comrades (the circumstances are described above in the text section 'Victoria Cross awards'). Simpson is depicted wearing a maroon beret with the brass 'Skippy' cap badge more commonly worn on the slouch hat or Service Dress cap.

C3: Captain Ian Teague

Captain Teague was instrumental in setting up the Revolutionary Development project in Quang Ngai Province. Many Team members acquired the US tropical combat uniform, here in its first pattern with shoulder straps and exposed pocket buttons. Teague has had a Vietnamese tailor embellish the coat with a range of unofficial insignia in black. US basic parachute wings are directly embroidered onto the left breast, with the Vietnamese equivalent on the right above his name. He wears both foreign wings in the prescribed positions, and though obscured here he probably has Australian wings on his right sleeve. (Later, as CO of 1 Sqn SASR, Teague had a batch of subdued black-on-green SASR wings made up locally for wear on JGs – a rare exception to the regiment's traditional disregard of insignia, unofficial or otherwise.) His rank 'pips', backed in infantry scarlet, are worn on detachable slides. On this occasion Teague wears the green Australian Commando Companies beret with its bi-metal dagger/boomerang badge.

C4: WO2 C.N.McEvoy, 1968

Depicted briefing members of a Mike Force patrol in June 1968, McEvoy uses hand signals to communicate with his Strikers. Over US tropical combat uniform he wears a Vietnamese-made rubberized rain parka in the monsoon weather – note that it is worn over his webbing, so will probably be removed when the patrol gets underway. The abbreviated equipment and lack of a pack indicate that this is a short-range clearing patrol within a few miles of the unit's perimeter rather than anything more lengthy. The short-brimmed 'tiger-stripe' jungle hat was popular among the Mike Forces, as were berets in the same pattern.

C5: WO2 E.C.Burns, 1970

Burns was an armour adviser to the ARVN 7th Cavalry Sqn in Quang Tri Province. He wears the traditional black Armoured Corps beret, with a unique combination of insignia: left of his own RAAC badge he has added the silver-wire embroidered badge of the Vietnamese Armoured Corps. Team members attached to armour units would also often wear the Vietnamese armour qualification badge on the right breast.

C6: WO2 S.F.Reid, 1972

Taken from a photograph showing Reid instructing Regional Forces, this shows the work/barracks uniform standardized for AATTV in the closing stages of the war. The 'tropical greens' shirt was the norm by 1972. Since the end of 1970 Team members had worn their name above the right pocket, occasionally with a matching 'AATTV' tape above the left; the AMF 'Rising Sun' patch was worn above the left sleeve pocket. Detachable brassards were popular for displaying other insignia: Vietnam's climate required frequent and rigorous laundering of JGs, and the sleeve pockets also made it difficult to sew the AATTV patch directly onto the shirt. On 10 June 1971, AATTV sent a request via Commander AFV to the AHQ Dress Committee for approval of the 'Beret, Rifle Green'; approval was given in December 1971, with the proviso that it was to be worn by Team members only while serving in Vietnam, as an optional item at their own expense. After initial efforts to find a local supplier of a sufficiently high quality item failed, in January 1972 the contract was placed with an established Australian firm, Latiners Pty Ltd of Victoria.

D: 'OTHER ARMS'

D1: Helicopter pilot, No.9 Squadron RAAF, 1968

Nine Squadron operated out of Vung Tau, flying in support of the Task Force from April 1966 to November 1971. Both RAAF and RAN pilots served tours, flying US UH-1 Iroquois 'Huey' helicopters; initially the squadron had eight aircraft, increasing to 16 at the height of operations during 1969. This pilot wears the universally issued Australian flightsuit of light sage green fire-retardant cotton, with a neck-to-crotch zip fastener and an assortment of pockets. Over this is worn a US 'Body Armor, Fragmentation, Small Arms Protective, Aircrewman' – popularly known as 'chicken plate'. Specifically designed for helicopter crews, these vests featured removable ceramic plates: pilots/co-pilots who sat in armoured seats required the front plate only; crew chiefs and gunners, who moved about in the aircraft exposing their backs, wore both. The vest underwent several modifications and is shown here in its final configuration, with shoulder adjustment and a nylon map pocket on the front plate. The flight helmet is an American AFH-1 'Crash Ballistic Protective Flying Helmet' introduced in 1965. Mostly painted plain green, they were occasionally seen with a nationally inspired insignia added – a small white Kiwi in the case of some New Zealand pilots. The majority of pilots carried a sidearm as personal protection, here a 9mm Browning in a Canadian-made holster; these were the most common holsters in Australian service, and featured a quick-release tab and spare magazine pocket.

D2: Tank commander, Royal Australian Armoured Corps, 1968

Based on a photograph of 2nd Lt Brian Sullivan, Troop Leader, 1 Tp, C Sqn, 1 Armd Regt, who would win a Military Cross for his part in the successful action at Binh Ba in June 1969. The usual armoured field dress was JGs – tanksuits were more typically worn in base areas. The black beret with the silver RAAC badge was a source of much pride to the 'turret-heads', being one of the few berets habitually worn on operations by Australians. The British '41' headset was part of the Centurion tank's internal communications equipment; Australians assigned to Cavalry units equipped with the American M113 APC used headsets appropriate to those vehicles.

D3: Gunner, 161 Battery, Royal New Zealand Artillery, 1966

One of the first New Zealanders to be deployed to Vietnam, this gunner wears the RNZA dark blue beret with traditional red-over-blue artillery backing to the badge. During their first tour 161 Bty initiated the purchase of black cotton cravats embroidered with a small white fern-leaf. These were worn as here with 'best' JGs for battery parades and other formal occasions, the JG shirt being further embellished with white-on-black national title slides.

D4: Pilot, AAAC, 1969

161 Reconnaissance Flight was the Australian Army's independent aviation unit in Vietnam, flying both helicopters and fixed wing aircraft. This captain wears embroidered rank and national titles on JG slides, and Army pilot's wings flat-embroidered on JG on the left breast. The AAAC's pale blue beret, with its silver badge on a black patch, is modelled on that of Britain's Army Air Corps. Most Australian corps based the design of their cap badge on the British originals, often with an additional Australian feature such as a boomerang or kangaroo.

D5: Trooper, 3rd Cavalry Regiment RAAC, 1969

The rotating squadrons from 3rd Cavalry Regt were 1ATF's armoured personnel carrier unit, operating US M113 APCs. Before the arrival of 1 Armd Regt's first Centurion heavy tanks the APCs were committed in a range of combat support roles

Machine gunner from a newly arrived New Zealand infantry company – see Plate E. The NZ shoulder titles and green 1RNZIR beret were worn at times when a show of national identity was desirable, e.g. during troop movements or in base areas, but never in the field. The half-buttoning British flannel shirt is worn with Australian-type 'tropical JG' trousers; the Australian M1956 webbing is supplemented with British 44 Pattern pouches. (NZ Army PR)

M113 crew of the original 1 APC Tp from 4th/19th Prince of Wales' Light Horse Regt; they wore the silver PoW feathers cap badge on the black RAAC beret until the troop was redesignated 1 APC Sqn in May 1966, taking the RAAC badge. The M1 helmet with WWII net, worn for this publicity shot, was rarely used by drivers in the field. (Neville Modystack)

for which they were not really equipped, but the troopers showed admirable aggressiveness. This driver is posed deliberately to illustrate a number of points of Cavalry dress and as such is somewhat theoretical, standard JGs being the more normal field uniform. The same flightsuit as worn by D1 was available to APC crews from 1968; while some individuals chose to wear it on operations the majority were kept as unofficial barracks dress, as one veteran recalls: 'JGs were worn for work and the flightsuit was put on at the end of the day to go to the boozer'. The US issue Combat Vehicle Crew (CVC) helmet was mainly worn by drivers and was never popular; the black RAAC beret with corps badge was the more common headgear, along with the occasional US or Vietnamese baseball cap. In 1965/66 some Australian APC crews had been issued with US APH-5 flying helmets as used in helicopters, converted to marry up with the vehicle comms system, but their use was limited. A pair of US 'sun, wind and dust goggles' are worn as protection from dust thrown up by the tracks. After the arrival in theatre of 1 Armd Regt's Centurions, Australian APCs began to fall victim to VC mines laid to destroy the heavy tanks. The effect of an anti-tank mine on the thinly armoured M113s was appalling, and the use of both CVC helmets and body armour increased among APC crews. Here a collarless US M1952 vest is worn, though M69 models were issued later; both types featured semi-flexible layers of nylon rather than the rigid plates of the helicopter armour. The Australian F1 sub-machine gun was the successor to the Owen; both were used in armoured units, being relatively short and manageable inside an AFV. Introduced in 1963, the F1 used the same 34-round curved magazine and 9mm ammunition as the British Sterling. Because the F1's magazine was placed above the barrel the sights had to be off-set in the same way as the Owen's; the cocking handle was placed on the left side so that, like the SLR, the weapon could be cocked without removing the hand from the pistol grip.

D6–D11: Vietnamese-made shoulder patches
These are based on examples in the Australian War Memorial collection. Such unofficial insignia were widely available throughout Vietnam and could be bought for a few piastres; Australian Army tolerance for such items was famously low, however, and their use was restricted to off-duty dress.

D6: 4 Troop, 1 Armoured Regiment
D7: 1 Tp, 1 Armd Regt
D8: 1 Tp, A Sqn, 3 Cav Regt
D9: A Sqn, 3 Cav Regt
D10: 3 Tp, 1 Armd Regt
D11: 161 Recce Flt, AAAC (one of several versions)

E: MID-WAR INFANTRY
E1: Grenadier, Victor 2 Company, 1 RNZIR, 1967
This Maori soldier wears Australian-pattern JGs and GP boots; at this stage the New Zealand contingent was almost totally reliant on 1ATF's supply system. The jungle hat is also still of British origin; NZ-manufactured 'greens' and hats were not yet in service. The unique black 'Kiwi' cravat was introduced by the original Victor 1 Co in 1967 and adopted by subsequent companies, most often worn as a sweat scarf as here, though occasionally around the jungle hat. Webbing is US M1956 belt, suspenders and 'universal' ammunition pouches with – typically – a pair of large 44 Pattern basic pouches on the hips; an M18 coloured smoke grenade hangs from the shoulder harness. The US M79 40mm grenade launcher – one of the most successful infantry weapons of the war – was dubbed the 'wombat gun' by the Kiwis, and each rifle section had a designated grenadier. The high explosive rounds effectively covered the area between the furthest range of a hand-thrown grenade and the middle range of a 60mm mortar. The section's grenadier would also carry an M16 rather than the heavier SLR.

E2: Private, Whiskey 1 Company, 1 RNZIR, 1968

Many members of 1RNZIR had served with 28th Commonwealth Bde in Malaysia, and the battalion's home was at Wellington Lines, Terendak Camp. The Kiwis were equipped from the British Q-stores and received sets of 44 Pattern webbing among other items of British origin. The British flannel shirts were especially popular, as they soaked up sweat and were warm at night; they were considered far superior to the Australian or NZ equivalents. This British equipment stayed in the New Zealand system and was much in evidence in Vietnam, the 44 Pattern webbing in particular being favoured over the US M1956 and later Australian equipment; it also lent something of an 'old sweat' air, which many Kiwis were keen to foster. Here a belt order of basic pouches and water bottle carriers is worn, with Australian M1956 plastic canteens; the suspenders were often discarded. The 44 Pattern haversack was the most commonly seen pack in New Zealand service until the ARVN rucksack and later Australian 'large pack' became available. An M72 LAW is secured beneath the pack flap; these single-use, throw-away weapons were designed to destroy armour but were found to be equally useful against enemy bunkers. A Whiskey 1 veteran recalls the demise of a VC who thought he was safe hiding behind a large ant-hill – a LAW destroyed both. New Zealand infantry would often add a chin cord to their jungle hats. The red diamond was worn on the left arm by all ranks of 1RNZIR and was awarded upon completion of Infantry Corps Training at Burnham; it was seen in Vietnam, but rarely.

E3: Signaller, 6RAR, 1970

Standard JGs are worn with an Australian-made jungle hat. From the outset Australian signallers had acquired the US 'lightweight rucksack and frame' for the carriage of the AN/PRC-25 FM receiver/transmitter; the nylon bag hung low on the aluminium frame, allowing the radio and other items to be strapped to the upper portion. The flexible tape antenna could be bent down when moving through heavy bush; the handset was simply hung from a convenient point on the webbing. Most Sigs carried a spares bag (here obscured beyond the '25 set') containing a back-up handset and the sectional 'fish-pole' antenna used when longer range was required. Webbing is M1956

with additional items attached to both rucksack and frame; because the Australians relied less heavily on air support the profusion of smoke grenades typically carried by American RTOs is absent.

E4: Private, Victor 1 Company, 1 Royal New Zealand Infantry Regiment, 1967

From a photograph of Pte V.Pyke. The green RNZIR beret was worn with the JG uniform for parades, transit moves, and around the lines at Nui Dat. The badge features a kiwi surrounded by fern-leaves over a scroll reading 'Onward'; Vietnam era examples were either anodized aluminium or the older white metal type with enamelled details – green riband, red centre.

E5: Unofficial patch, Whiskey 1 Company, 1 RNZIR

F: SPECIAL AIR SERVICE

F1: Patrol member, 3 Squadron SASR, 1969

This trooper wears the US ERDL uniform with US 'J-boots', and a Vietnamese-made 'tiger-stripe' beret. The SAS patrol gloves typically have the fingers cut off, allowing full use of the weapon while still protecting the hands; even minor cuts and abrasions would soon turn septic in the tropical environment. Based on the US Nomex pilot gloves, the SAS version was made from a breathable cotton mesh with leather rein-forcement to the palm and trigger-finger. The belt kit is a typical mix of M1956 components, apart from the low-slung ammunition pouch at front right. These pouches – unique to SASR, and made for the regiment by a firm in Perth – were originally designed and ordered by 1 Sqn and paid for from unit funds. Two distinct variations existed: the more common M16 pouch, and a larger type for SLR magazines. The M16 version, based on the 44 Pattern in use by Britain's 22 SAS Regt, was a double pouch which hung from a simple wide belt loop and closed with a quick-release tab. In 1968 the Australian squadron in Vietnam requested a similar pouch for the larger 20-round SLR magazines, also with a simple belt loop which allowed the pouch to be worn in two positions on the belt. The larger 30-round magazines were

In January 1967 the expanded APC unit became A Sqn, 3rd Cavalry Regiment. Here, during Operation 'Blue Mountains' in July 1968, Sgt Dave Brooks of A Sqn wears the newly issued 'tropical JGs'. American CVC helmets were unpopular, being hot, heavy, restricting the hearing, and causing heat rash and ear infections; besides, the black RAAC beret was a jealously guarded 'tribal' headgear for both Cavalry and 'Tankies'. The US headset, with its boom microphone, eliminated the need for a handset; the small box housing the transmit switch hung around the neck, and is visible in Brooks' right hand.

Spring 1971: a 2 Sqn SASR patrol member expresses his appreciation at being photographed – his relaxed air and lack of headgear suggests that the patrol is over and an LZ is being secured for helicopter extraction. Of particular interest is the barely recognizable M60 machine gun reconstructed in the squadron workshop – see Plate G4. The handguards and bipod have been removed, the barrel shortened, and an SLR pistol grip has been added off-set half way along the barrel.

generally carried in 44 Pattern basic pouches. The pack carried here is the US 'tropical rucksack', essentially an enlarged nylon version of the ARVN rucksack. It featured three small external pockets and had an integral sprung steel X-frame. On his right shoulder harness are taped a US aircrew survival knife and a strobe light in its cover. The small aluminium canisters taped to the left suspender are 'mini smoke grenades', carried by all patrol members and used as a last resort signalling device when the supply of M18 smoke grenades had been expended. The SLR has been subjected to a range of SAS modifications: the flash suppressor, bayonet lugs, sling swivels and carrying handle have been removed, an additional pistol grip is attached to the handguard, and the whole weapon – including the 30-rd magazine – has been lavishly camouflage-painted.

F2: Patrol member, 2 Squadron SASR, 1971
The M203 rifle/grenade launcher combination was ideally suited to the SASR's small but heavily armed patrols; the only modifications here are the removal of sling swivels and flash suppressor. The weapon's 40mm grenade rounds were usually carried in six-pocket bandoliers or in the US issue grenadier's vest; 2 Sqn devised the purpose-made rig illustrated here,

featuring two vertical rows of five pockets on a sleeve that fitted over the shoulder harness. A surviving example is on display at the Australian War Memorial, along with the rest of the field gear belonging to Don Barnby of 2 Sqn; photographs also show its use by other squadron members in 1971. The smaller twin-pocket SAS M16 ammunition pouches are worn low on the belt; SAS preference has always been for the simple belt loop system that eliminates all clumsy metal fittings, and standard pouches were often modified accordingly. The British-made green/brown camouflage netting sniper veil was often seen in SAS service alongside the plain green Australian type. Headbands were popular, since they soaked up sweat without impairing hearing or vision; however, men with lighter coloured hair had to opt for a more concealing jungle hat or beret.

F3: Corporal, 2 Squadron SASR, 1971
Corporal Ian Rasmussen of F Tp, 2 Sqn wears 'best' JGs with the regiment's sand-coloured beret, here the Australian issue version made by Beret Mnfrs Pty Ltd of Victoria, with a matching colour headband rather than the more usual black. Privately purchased berets were also commonly seen, including a lightweight version by Christies of Sydney which had a black synthetic sweatband and was unlined for hot climates. British-made berets with black leather sweatbands were also popular. Unlike the British, all ranks of SASR wear a brass or bi-metal badge on a black felt backing shield; like the berets, these badges were from a variety of manufacturers, the most common during the Vietnam era being a British 'Stabrite' anodized type. Insignia permitted on the JG shirt was the same as prescribed for the tan summer uniform; note that there was no JG version of the SASR parachute wings, and the embroidered summer wings on tan backing are worn. Brass national titles were either pinned straight through the shoulder straps or worn on removable slides. The SASR lanyard worn on the left shoulder is in 'Garter blue'.

F4: Patrol member, 2 Squadron SASR, 1971
This trooper wears a locally procured short-brim jungle hat in lightweight 'tiger-stripe' fabric. The ARVN rucksack was a favourite with all Anzac troops and was known as the 'Ranger pack' in SAS use. Designed for troops who averaged only 5ft 2ins and 125lbs, it was lightweight and compact and rode tight to the back; a 2 Sqn file of 1969 notes that an ideal SAS pack should not be so wide as to impede movement through heavy jungle, and requests the issue of 'Ranger packs' to the squadron. The belt kit is a typical mix, all items being modified with wide belt loops: at the front is an Australian M1956 'large' ammunition pouch with a sharpening stone in a small leather pocket stitched to the side; next is a 44 Pattern basic pouch, one of the only types large enough to hold 30-rd SLR magazines; and at the rear are a 44 Pattern 'water bottle' cover and an Australian M1956 'canteen' cover, the former with a green Australian-made and the latter with a browner US-made plastic canteen. A further Australian M1956 canteen is added to the side of the pack; water was a precious commodity on the lengthy SAS patrols. Webbing, pack, face and weapon have been thoroughly camouflaged. The SLR is one of the 'carbine' versions produced by the squadron armourer; some had a simple 'barrel-chop', but some, as here, were extensively reworked. The barrel, gas return and handguard have been shortened significantly; the flash suppressor has

been replaced in this instance; a 30-rd magazine is fitted, and a field dressing has been taped to the butt.

G: SPECIAL AIR SERVICE

G1: Patrol member, 4 Troop NZSAS, 1970

Based on a series of photographs of a New Zealand patrol in late 1970, this trooper wears the ERDL uniform, US 'J-boots', and a locally-made jungle hat with the brim shortened and a random camouflage pattern applied. Though jungle hats in a variety of patterns were available it was common SAS practice to camouflage-paint a plain green one to individual preference. Belt kit is M1956 with the SAS M16 ammunition pouches; note the large belt loops which allow the pouch to hang well below waist level. On the shoulder harness are taped a strobe light in its case and two mini smoke grenades; an M67 'baseball' grenade hangs from the side of one ammunition pouch. The grenade carrier vest for the XM148's 40mm rounds is based on a surviving example, daubed with camouflage paint. These US-made vests, constructed in nylon with mesh back and shoulder areas for ventilation, were commonly used by SAS men armed with rifle/grenade-launcher combos. Originally the vest incorporated three rows of pockets, the lower two for 40mm HE and the upper for the longer illumination rounds, but as the latter were rarely used on SAS patrols these pockets have been removed. The SAS issue 'Bergan' rucksack was worn well into the 1970s, here an older example with brass fittings; though many considered it

outdated and opted for more contemporary packs, the Bergan was something of an SAS trademark. The XM148 grenade launcher attached to an M16A1 rifle was trialled by 3 Sqn in 1966 and quickly adopted by SASR, as was its M203 upgrade. This example has been modified by a simple barrel-chop to maximise noise and flash; a grab-sling improvised from para-cord allows the weapon to be recovered if its owner becomes a casualty.

G2: Patrol member, 1 Squadron SASR, 1968

Initially some sets of 'tiger-stripe' uniform were purchased locally for SASR. In 1968 the resident squadron submitted evaluations of the 'tiger-stripes' and the US ERDL pattern; although the latter won out on most points and was put forward for adoption, some SAS men continued to favour the local pattern. The evaluation judged it good for primary

April 1971: No.25 Patrol, F Tp, 2 Sqn SASR – see Plates F & G. All wear ERDL camouflage uniform, with netting sweat scarves and (though hidden here) US jungle boots. Webbing is the usual M1956 with SAS additions. Trooper Don Barnby (second left) wears the unique 40mm grenade pouch harness – see Plate F2 – and carries the M16/XM148 rifle/grenade launcher combination. The trooper at rear right has the US grenadier's vest, with the upper row of pockets for the longer illumination rounds removed. At front left, note the US 'Ka-Bar' knife taped to the harness, and the 'chopped' SLR with additional off-set forward pistol grip.

Saigon, May 1968: WO2 Danny Neville DCM, of SASR, photographed before going on 'R & R'. The tan summer shirt and khaki polyester trousers were only used in transit, when a smart appearance was demanded, and were worn with the slouch hat or an appropriate beret. The Australian-made sand-coloured SAS beret had a matching head band; as was common among longer-serving members, Neville's seems to be a British example with a black leather band. The fine variations of cap badge manufacture are a study in themselves; Neville's is bi-metal, on a black felt patch. The shoulder straps bear brass 'Australia' titles on removable slides (unit-specific titles – 'SAS', 'RAR', etc – were only to be worn in Australia); and note the SASR's blue lanyard on the left shoulder. In British and 'old Commonwealth' armies a double row of medal ribbons indicates long and active service; the Distinguished Conduct Medal is a gallantry decoration second only to the VC. WO2 Neville served a total of five years in Vietnam between 1963 and 1971, mostly with AATTV. Out of shot are his crown badge of rank, worn on both upper sleeves, and the flat-embroidered blue/white SAS parachute wings worn on the upper right sleeve (see Plate F3).

jungle but not for more open areas, especially bamboo, due to the horizontally striped pattern; its cut was also considered too tight and its pockets too small. Among many alternatives sought for the Bergan rucksack (including examples made in Thailand, Singapore, Malaysia and other Asian countries where SASR operated), the pack illustrated is based on a British 44 Pattern haversack but larger and with deeper side pockets; examples studied are made of lightweight webbing with typically poor-quality Asian metal fittings. Belt kit consists of the usual mix of M1956 and 44 Pattern items. On SAS belt order a single M1956 pouch was often used for a survival/aid kit – each patrol member assembled his own, from a range of first-aid and escape/evasion items. The kit was always worn on the webbing, which was never taken off during a patrol, so was always to hand even if the rucksack had to be dropped. In late 1967, SASR requested nine L34A1 Patchett (Sterling) silenced SMGs from England. The squadron in Vietnam had reported that several recce-ambush patrols had been compromised prematurely due to contacts; it was felt that if given the means to remove single or small groups of enemy silently, patrols would be able to continue with their missions. The L34A1 was considered ideal for this task and would remain in SASR service – though one veteran recalls them being mainly used for sniping at monkeys, and the tyres of Military Police Landrovers, from SAS Hill at Nui Dat... .

G3: Trooper, 4 Troop NZSAS, 1969
From December 1968 the NZSAS contributed a troop to the Australian squadron at Nui Dat; in normal circumstances a troop was 12 strong, but in Vietnam this was increased to

26 men. Unlike the Australians, NZSAS wore a maroon beret with the British-made embroidered badge – for officers, a wire-embroidered version. The Australian 'camouflage raincoat' was occasionally worn around base areas during the monsoon. Dubbed the 'Can't See Me' coat, this knee-length garment was made from rubber-coated fabric overprinted with an irregular brown 'splotch' camouflage pattern; it incorporated a shoulder cape modelled on that of the traditional outback drover's coat. Of dubious value, the coats could be traded with Americans, with whom they were popular; a matching jungle hat was made but rarely seen in use.

G4: Patrol member, 3 Squadron SASR, 1967
The M60 was another weapon modified by SAS armourers. The most visible alteration is the reduction in barrel length, achieved by removing the section that incorporates both foresight and bipod bracket, the flash suppressor being replaced further back. The plastic handguard and bipod legs have been removed and a forward pistol grip added; together with the improvised sling, this improved the overall balance and allowed the weapon to be fired from the hip. The Australian Bergan rucksack was based on that used by the British Army and had changed little from its WWII design: a simple canvas bag with three external pockets, carried on a steel A-frame. The Australian version made at the Commonwealth Government Clothing Factory (CGCF) differed only in the materials used: olive green canvas with tan webbing straps, and all buckles and fittings of blackened metal. Webbing is British 44 Pattern water bottles, US M1956 suspenders and ammunition pouches, the latter with two M18 coloured smoke grenades hung from the side loops.

H: ROYAL AUSTRALIAN REGIMENT, 1969–72
H1: Private, 6RAR, 1969
This National Service rifleman is dressed and equipped entirely in items of Australian origin, in contrast to his predecessors. The 'tropical' or 'combat greens' were widely

issued by this stage, although the original pattern was still in use concurrently. The tropical JG trousers were obviously influenced by the US equivalent, but the thigh pockets were positioned too far to the front and were much less capacious. Likewise the shirt sleeve pockets, intended to take a field dressing, were more often used to carry packets of cigarettes. The jungle hat is the Australian version with small ventilator eyelets and slightly larger brim. Webbing is Australian-made M1956 in the configuration specified in the 'Soldier's Handbook'. The large ammunition pouches are worn on the belt in the same manner as the smaller US originals, and are additionally clipped to the shoulder suspenders. A field dressing/compass case was often attached to one ammunition pouch, and a toggle rope hangs from the other. An Australian-made machete is worn on the belt in its canvas sheath complete with a small external pocket for a sharpening stone, and here has a field dressing taped to the end. A belt of 7.62mm MG link is draped around the torso protected by the usual plastic sleeve. The SLR has the parkerized finish, green plastic carrying handle and oval-section handguard of later production Australian weapons; the plastic handle was introduced in 1968, as the earlier wooden handles were prone to breaking off.

H2: Private, 3RAR, 1971
This forward scout of the Third Battalion ('Old Faithful') gives the hand signal for 'section commander up' – two fingers representing corporal's stripes, held against the sleeve. Even this late in the war the standard JGs were worn on operations and were preferred by many over the more tightly tailored 'tropical' version. Webbing is all Australian M1956: a pair of ammunition pouches on each hip and several canteens at the rear (note that while the pouches are stamped with the Ordnance arrow the canteen covers are unmarked). Slung under the arm is the Australian version of the 2-quart collapsible water bladder. Modelled on the US type, this comprised a clear vinyl bladder in an outer cover with both belt loops and a shoulder sling; the cover was made from the distinctive Australian green/brown camouflage rubberized fabric also used for the 'individual shelter carrier', and as a waterproof lining in both the large ammunition pouches and the pack. The 'Field Pack, Canvas, Olive Drab, 18in x 14in x 7in' (usually called simply the 'large pack') was well established by the early 1970s, although it would never totally replace the many US packs in Australian use. The larger bottom compartment, which made the most contact with the wearer's back, was meant for 'soft kit' such as the sleeping gear; the upper portion contained 'hard kit' like rations and radios. The Australian M1956 entrenching tool cover was introduced around the same time as the pack

Operation 'Petrie', July 1970: Pte Nicholas Andropof of 8RAR provides a typical image of a Digger in the late stages of the war. A mismatched set of standard JG shirt and tropical trousers is worn with a British hat. Webbing is Australian M1956 ammunition pouches and canteens hung low on the rear of the belt, with a British 44 Pattern basic pouch on the hip. Secured to the rucksack frame is an ARVN rucksack with its two external pockets; additional items including M1956 canteens are attached to both frame and rucksack. The 66mm M72 LAW was often found useful against static enemy positions, frequently encountered in the rubber plantations of Phuoc Tuy.

and is worn here in the prescribed position; the light green canvas cover lacks the bayonet attachment of the US original. The folding M1961 'Combination Entrenching Tool' was also manufactured in Australia as a direct copy of the US type.

H3: Private, 8RAR, 1970
'The Grey Eight' conducted Operation 'Hammersley' during February–March 1970 in the Long Hai hills. This established VC staging area was known to be heavily mined, and a battalion issue was made of both steel helmets and body armour. Photographs of the operation show helmets worn both with and without netting covers in roughly equal proportions. Though Australia manufactured the M1 helmet there was no Australian equivalent of the camouflage cloth cover worn by American troops; instead older netting covers were issued, or were fabricated from a length of Australian sweat scarf, as here. The US 'Body Armor, Fragmentation Protective Vest with Three Quarter Collar, M69' was an upgraded version of the earlier M52 incorporating a semi-stiff collar with the same ballistic filling as the torso. Both types of vest were hot and restrictive, and were only worn by Australian infantry when the mine threat was considered greater than usual. Webbing is Australian M1956, although photographs taken during 'Hammersley' show that many members of 8RAR retained 37/44 Pattern basic pouches even at this date.

INDEX

Figures in **bold** refer to illustrations

161st Battery Royal New Zealand Artillery 10
173rd Airborne Brigade (US) 9, 10, 11, 19

Armitpage, Private Nicholas 62
ANZAC forces
    chronology of operations 14–15
    glossary of terms 48–9, 51
    integration of 17, 18
    operational methods 19–21
    personnel relations 10–11
    unit composition 20–1
    usage of acronym 3
ANZAC Training Teams **C**, 55–6
ANZUS Brigade 9, 11, 19
ANZUS Treaty (1951) 4, 5
Army of the Republic of Vietnam (ARVN) 6, 19
Australia, New Zealand and US (ANZUS)
    Treaty (1951) 4, 5
Australian and New Zealand
    foreign policy 4, 5
Australian and New Zealand Special Air Service
    (SAS and NZSAS) 10, 13, 23–5
    camouflage 24–5
    equipment 25, 47–8
    firepower 24
    troopers **24, 25, 51, 60, 61**
    uniforms **F, G,** 46–50, **47, 50,** 59–62
    weaponry **52**
Australian Army Training Team Vietnam (AATTV)
    5, **6**, 7, **7**, 8, **B,** 54–5
    insignia **B6,** 46
Australian National Service Conscripts 13
Australian Order of Battle 16
Australian Task Force (1ATF) 11–13, 19
    independence of 11–12
    Long Tan action 22–3

Badcoe, Major Peter 9
Barnby, Trooper Dave **25, 61**
Bien Hoa airbase **3,** 4, 9, **9**
Blundell, Private Jim **14**
Borneo 4, 5, 10, 18
Boyd, Private Ron 22
Briggs, Corporal Ivor **41**
Britain, involvement in South East Asia 4
Brooks, Sergeant Dave **59**
Brumfield, Lieut. Colonel Ivan 9
Buckney, Sergeant Peter **21**
Burns, Warrant Officer 2 E.C. **C5,** 56

Central Intelligence Agency (CIA) 7
Clarke, Captain Rex **6, B2,** 54
Communism in South East Asia 3–4
Cowburn, Trooper Tom **14**

Delahunty, Captain N.F. **7**
Dewonkowski, Private Jan **27**
Domino Theory 4

Edwards, Sergeant K.A. **6**
Eisenhower, Dwight D., 34th President of the
    United States 4
Elliott, Private Ralph 15

France, involvement in South East Asia 4

Gebhardt, Sergeant John **47, 49**
Gill, Warrant Officer 2 M. 8
Goldspink, Lieutenant Ross **12**
grenadier **E1,** 58
gunner **D3,** 57

Halls, Corporal Brian **28**
helicopter, OH-13 Sioux (Possum) **12**

helicopter pilot **D1,** 57

Ilsley, Private Graham **43**
Indonesia 4
insignia **D, E5,** 45, 45–6, **46,** 58, 59
    Australian Army Training Team shoulder and
      beret badge **B6, B7,** 55
    Australian military forces patch **A1,** 54

Jackson, Brigadier O.D. 12, 13
Jarratt, Captain P. **B4,** 54
Johnson, Lyndon B., 36th President of the
    United States 3
jungle-greens (JG's) *see* uniforms: jungle-greens

Kelly, Warrant Officer 2 A.M. 9
Kirby, Sergeant Mervyn **26**

Lichtwark, Warrant Officer 2 Brian **C1,** 55
Long Tan action 22–3
Lyons, Lieutenant Trevor **10**

M60 machine gun **60**
M113 armoured vehicle crew **58**
McAuley, Corporal Lex **19**
McCloskey, Warrant Officer 2 A.B. **B5,** 54–5
McEvoy, Warrant Officer 2 C.N. **C4,** 56
McGarry, Warrant Officer 2 L.G. **7**
machine gunner **57**
Malaya and Malaysia 4, 18
Menzies, Robert, Prime Minister of Australia 5, 9
military advisers 5–9
Military Assistance Advisory Group (MAAG) 5
Military Assistance Command Vietnam (MACV) 6
Milwood, Sergeant Robert **27**
Montagnard 'strikers' **6**
munitions 42–3
Murphy, Lieutenant Mick **29**

Neville, Warrant Officer 2 Danny **62**
New Zealand
    and conscription 18
New Zealand Army Detachment Vietnam
    (NZADVN or NEWZAD) 5
New Zealand M60 gun team **18**
New Zealand rifleman **17**
New Zealand Special Air Service (NZSAS) *see*
    Australian and New Zealand Special Air Service
North Vietnamese Army (NVA) **26**
Nui Dat 12, 13, 20, **20,** 22, 23

OH-13 Sioux (Possum) helicopter **12**
O'Keefe, Sergeant John **50**
operations
    contrasting methods of US and ANZACs 19–20
    Long Tan action 22–3

paratroops 9, 10, 11, 19
patrol scout (NZ) **16**
Payne, Warrant Officer 2 Keith **8,** 9
Petersen, Captain Barry 7
Phuoc Tuy Province 12
pilot **D4,** 57
Priestley, Private John **26**
privates
    infantry **E2, E4,** 59
    Royal Australian Regiment (RAR) **A1, H,**
      53, 62–3

radio communication **14, 47**
rations 42
Reid, Warrant Officer 2 S.F. **C6,** 56
Rodgers, Trooper Stephen **50**
Roy, Warrant Officer 2 J.D. **B3,** 54
Royal Australian Air Force (RAAF) **11**
Royal Australian Armoured Corps (RAAC) **5**
Royal Australian Regiment (RAR) **3,** 4, 9, **A,** 53–4
    1st Battalion 9, 10, 11

2nd Battalion 17
5th Battalion 12, 13
6th Battalion 13
    D Company 22–3
    uniforms **A, H,** 53–4, 62–3
Royal New Zealand Artillery 10
Royal New Zealand Infantry Regiment (RNZIR)
    17, 18
    V (Victor 1) Company 17, 18
    W (Whiskey 1) Company 17

Sharp, Lieutenant Gordon 22–3
Shennan, Warrant Officer 2 W. **B1,** 54
signaller **E3,** 59
Simpson, Warrant Officer 2 R.S. 7, 8–9, **C2,** 55–6
Smith, Major Harry 23
South East Asian Treaty Organization
    (SEATO) 4, 9
South Vietnamese Army 5
Special Air Service (SAS) *see* Australian and New
    Zealand Special Air Service (SAS and NZSAS)
Swanton, Warrant Officer 2 Ron 8

tank commander **D2,** 57
Teague, Captain I.C. **7, C3,** 56
troopers
    crewman cavalry **D5,** 57–8
    Special Air Service (SAS) **G3,** 62

uniforms *see also* insignia; webbing
    Australian 25–9
    footwear 28–9, **55**
    grenadier **E1,** 58
    gunner **D3,** 57
    headgear 27–8, **54**
    helicopter pilot **D1,** 57
    infantry **E2, E4,** 59
    jungle-greens (JG's) 5, 6, 10, 14, 17, 22, 26,
      27–9, **28, 29, 43, 53, 59**
    M60 machine gunner, Royal Australian
      Regiment (RAR) **A2,** 53
    New Zealand 43–5, **44**
    pilot **D4,** 57
    privates
      infantry **E2, E4,** 59
      Royal Australian Regiment (RAR) **A1, H,** 53
      62–3
    signaller **E3,** 59
    Special Air Service (SAS) **F, G,** 46–50, **47, 50,**
      59–62
    Staff Sergeant Royal Australian Regiment (RAR)
      A3, 53–4
    tank commander **D2,** 57
    troopers
      crewman cavalry **D5,** 57–8
      Special Air Service (SAS) **G3,** 62
United States
    foreign policy in Vietnam 3
United States Special Forces 7

Victoria Cross awards 8–9
Viet Cong 7, 8, 12, 22, 25, 26
Vietnam War
    Australian involvement in 3, 4
Vietnamese Ranger forces 6
Vietnamese Regional Forces (RFs) 6
Vietnamization 7–8
Vung Tau 12

weaponry **52, 56, 60**
webbing 29–32, 41–3, 53–63
    Australian modified M1956 30–1, **31, 32, 42**
    British 1937 and 1944 patterns 31–2, 41–2
    US M1956 29–30, **30, 41**
Westmoreland, General William 12
Wheatley, Warrant Officer 2 Kevin 'Dasher' 8, 9
White, Major Peter **10**